THIS GOOD NEWS

He then gave them the key to the understanding of the Scriptures. "This," he said to
them, "is the gist of the Scriptures: the
Messias must suffer and on the third day rise
from the dead.

"Furthermore: in his name the need of a
change of heart and forgiveness of sins must
be preached to all the nations; the preaching
must begin in Jerusalem, and you are the
witnesses of all this."

Luke 24, 45–48

THIS GOOD NEWS is one of the volumes in a series, IMPACT
BOOKS, designed to bring to the modern reader the significant
achievements of scholars, both Catholic and non-Catholic, in the
fields of Scripture, Theology, Philosophy, Mathematics, History,
and the Physical and Social Sciences. IMPACT BOOKS will explore these realms of human knowledge in order to give the average
man some idea of the work being carried on today within them
and in order to lay a basis for fruitful dialogue between men of
different interests and persuasions on questions vital to all mankind.

This Good News

An Introduction to
THE CATHOLIC THEOLOGY OF
THE NEW TESTAMENT

by QUENTIN QUESNELL, S.J.

THE BRUCE PUBLISHING COMPANY • *Milwaukee*

IMPRIMI POTEST:
John J. Foley, S.J.

NIHIL OBSTAT:
John A. Schulien, S.T.D.
Censor librorum

IMPRIMATUR:
✛ William E. Cousins
Archbishop of Milwaukee
December 10, 1963

Introduction

THIS book has a very limited aim. It will not be a general introduction to the New Testament. It will not try to explain what
the New Testament is, where it comes from, who wrote it, how
it was gathered together, or how it has come down to us. These
are all important topics, and anyone who wants to understand
what the New Testament is really saying must give some time to
studying them. But there already exist many good introductions
to the New Testament, such as Wikenhauser's *New Testament
Introduction,* which can be used for this purpose.

This book will be rather an introduction to the theology of the
New Testament; that is, it will try to communicate a simple outline of the central ideas of the New Testament proclamation and
teaching about God and our way to Him through and in our
Lord Jesus Christ.

First of all, then, it is only an introduction, an outline, a sketch,
It is not the whole story by any means. How could it be? Whole
volumes and series of volumes have been dedicated to the theology
of one or the other New Testament writer alone. A general theology
of the New Testament would have to rest upon the conclusions
of all those individual studies, as well as upon the conclusions
of additional thousands of books and articles devoted to exact,
line-by-line exegesis of the texts. It could not possibly be com-
pressed into a few hundred pages.

The fact that this is only an introduction implies that this cannot possibly be the last word on the subject. In fact the current
state of progress of biblical theology itself makes it impossible
that any book written at this time should hope or claim to be the

last word. The perfectly satisfactory detailed exegesis of every word in the New Testament which a completely satisfactory biblical theology would presuppose does not yet exist. The complete and satisfactory individual "theologies" of every single New Testament author have not yet been elaborated. Our knowledge of the history of New Testament times is still in progress, as is our understanding of the Church and the history of dogma.

But on the other hand, just because Scripture scholars and theologians are working constantly on exegesis and biblical theology, a certain point in the progress toward perfect understanding has been reached. It is not a static point; such things never are. New discoveries of real importance are being made all the time. Often enough these discoveries make it necessary to modify somewhat every general explanation written previously. Nevertheless, we do stand at a certain definite point along the line of progress, studies in biblical theology are at some one real stage at the moment. This book wants to do nothing more than give a picture of that moment; to sketch a picture, not of a finished theology, but of the shape and pattern which that theology seems to be taking today in the thinking of many different specialized workers.

Because this book is only an introduction, written above all for people who are not themselves doing professional work in the field, it has seemed better, because clearer, to attempt drawing this picture without actually recounting the many different current opinions and approaches in their diversity, without even trying to discuss the many disputes which are going on within the field. It has seemed more profitable to concentrate on those elements which, being common to many, have made any sort of discussion and argument possible in the first place.

For one cannot avoid noticing how a real consensus is coming about within the realm of theology strictly so-called, in spite of deep divergences on many of the underlying points of methods of interpretation and history. We shall try to reflect that consensus wherever possible. Where no consensus has been achieved, or where a consensus is, because of doctrinal commitments, unlikely or impossible, we shall simply follow the norm of Catholic teaching.

Our aim here then is not to innovate, but to sum up work which has been done and is being done. Of course even such a summary implies some innovation. Not every individual worker, for example, will willingly grant that his own school has common theological points of agreement with certain others. That is only another reason for not trying to demonstrate the agreements point by point with lists of names. Nor will all be willing by any means to grant that their work is tending intrinsically and of its own momentum toward Catholic truth.

That brings us to the need for a word of caution. This attempt to summarize current work and progress is and can be only an attempt, an experiment. In this field, as in all other scientific research, what we have called its present shape and form is in reality often only a tendency, a direction, a striving toward a certain future shape and form. The author sees the goal toward which biblical theology strives, as actually present in the teaching of the Catholic Church. But the theology is at present imperfect, even as our understanding of the details of the New Testament is imperfect. Therefore the attempt to sum up that reality in these pages will be of necessity imperfect and incomplete. The reader is asked to beware of the error of "only" — the feeling that any affirmative statement that such and such is true actually means to imply that such and such is the whole truth and the only truth. Nothing in this book has that meaning. We claim, for example, that the Apostles' Creed is central in Catholic teaching. That must not be taken as implying that the Nicene Creed, with its additional explanatory phrases, is not equally central. This danger of the "only" is a built-in difficulty for all theology. We know that all truth is in the Church, but, at any one moment, theology has not yet succeeded in putting it all into words.

Again, if we are to present here a structure which will help the reader to go on to further reading, thinking, and theologizing on his own, we have to find a central point or points around which to organize the structure. The very idea of a theology demands this too, for theology means understanding, and understanding demands or tends toward unity. But if we are to present everything as growing out from a center, then the early chapters must contain only implicitly the things which in later chapters will be unfolded from that one center. But that means that the statements of the early chapters will be still more imperfect, more liable to misunderstanding from the point of view of "only."

How are we to determine this central point from which our work will proceed? This is precisely the question which is most important of all and in the fields of philosophy and theology ordinarily gives rise to the greatest and longest disputes. Fortunately in the case of biblical theology, this happens to be the point on which the greatest consensus has been reached in recent years. Modern scripture research has tended more and more to join Catholic tradition as expressed in the Creeds, the sign of the cross, the heart of the mass, in seeing as the central point of New Testament theology that which in the New Testament itself is called the message, the preaching or *kerygma*, the gospel, the good news. Hence our title: THIS GOOD NEWS.

Of course the Catholic already possesses this message. He is familiar with its outline from the Apostles' Creed. He finds it in the catechism. He experiences it in the day-to-day preaching and life of the Church all his life through. Yet, coming to him as a normal part of everyday Catholic life, it comes as adapted in a special way to his peculiar needs here and now; it does not always come as a clearly defined message in so many explicit words. He may have learned to live by it — but never consciously and deliberately formulated it in his own mind. He may not be able to explain to a nonbeliever just what "good news" he and his Church have to offer. He may not have realized as yet how to use what he does know of the good news to help him mine the treasures of wisdom and knowledge hidden in the Old and New Testaments. He may not fully appreciate why joy, thanksgiving, and peace are such typically Christian virtues. He may, in reading the Bible and even in daily life as a Catholic, get so taken up with this or that small detail or aspect of the Church's practice and teaching that he somehow fails to perceive in anything like their full meaning the central truths which the Bible and the living Church are trying to present to him. If so, he necessarily misses much of the significance in the fact that the Church preserves the Bible for him as the word of God, that the Church is the best and ultimately the only interpreter of the Bible, that the Church is the Bible brought to life.

All this implies that a right understanding of the good news should have definite results in the personal lives of those who read the New Testament in its light. And so it should. A biblical theology does aim at bringing out religious values which are to be found in the New Testament by one who reads it faithfully, presupposing some previous grasp on his part of certain necessary introductory material.

It isn't that the New Testament cannot bring out its own values, far better than any commentator or system-builder can hope to do. An hour spent in the sincere attempt to read the New Testament, listening for God's word in it, will be far more profitable than many hours listening to or studying someone else's reflections on what the New Testament is trying to say. That is why the Church grants an indulgence for reading scripture itself; there are no indulgenced commentaries or biblical theology textbooks.

The New Testament can speak for itself. And more often than not it does so. The problem of remoteness, of strangeness, though real enough, does not make itself felt in the New Testament to the extent that it does in the Old. No one, even two thousand years later, reads the gospels completely unmoved. Even in passages which most ordinary readers no longer really understand in themselves, long years of association and familiarity have built up connotations and religious implications which come through to the reader in spite of all obstacles. One has heard them read in church. One has heard them referred to in long or short quotations, in direct and indirect references and allusions, in English literature, in the family circle, in homely proverbs. Religious ideas, inspirations, and values leap out at one from every page.

This is, of course, all to the good. And yet, good as it is, it has its own dangers. For, in the first place, many of the associations which long years of Christian living have connected with certain texts for this individual or that are, objectively speaking, not in the inspired text at all. One is actually bringing them in from outside. Hearing the sacred words, then, one remembers one's parents, or a certain talented preacher, or a slogan or motto of a club one once belonged to. One hears echoes of other things which are not the pure word of God as received and passed on in Catholic tradition, but interpretations, modifications, applications, special slants and outlooks which represent this or that individual school of spirituality, this or that individual Christian philosophy of life. Each of these may be good in itself. All of them are Christian. But they are not the inspired word of God. And they are certainly not *central*.

For these reasons we shall try to stress as much as possible this center of the Christian Faith, out from which all the rest grows and upon which it always all depends. This should help to a sharper vision and a firmer possession of the religious values of the New Testament. And this should help to a better understanding of the New Testament as well. For we can get at the meaning of the individual New Testament writings today only by reconstructing as much as possible in our own minds the ideas and concerns which were central for those who wrote it. If one message, kerygma, good news, gospel, dominated the thinking and preaching of the apostolic Church, then that means every page of the New Testament will yield more of its true sense the more it is read explicitly in the light of that central message.

Finally, we hope that such an approach to uncovering the thought of the New Testament writers, such an attempt to see in their true proportions the chief interests of the first-century Church, will also help Catholics of today to a clearer insight into the problems and concerns of the Church of our own time, occupied as she always is with the same basic concern as she was then: proclaiming and teaching about God and our way to him through our Lord Jesus Christ.

Contents

THE WORD IN THE
WORD INCARNATE

THE WORD IN THE
BODY OF CHRIST

POSTSCRIPT

THE WORD IN THE PREACHING

CHAPTER 1

What Is This Good News?

"GOSPEL" is "gōd-spell," an old English word for an old Greek word, and both of them mean "good news." That much we all learned in school long ago. Gospel is a name and a reality with which we all feel rather familiar from our earliest years. There is the gospel as we hear it read at mass every Sunday, some short little story from the life of Christ, usually bristling with pharisees and publicans, lepers and apostles, miracles and wonderful — though sometimes very mysterious — sayings of our Lord. There are the "four gospels," four books of the New Testament, which retreat masters often exhort us to take up and read through from beginning to end at least once in our lifetime. We know they tell the full story of the life of Jesus from the points of view of four different people who either knew him personally or were very close to someone who did.

The four gospels, we also know, are by Matthew, Mark, Luke, and John. We stand when parts of them are read aloud to us in church. They contain, in the words and actions of our Lord, the truths of faith which are most important of all to us. The Church appeals to them and to the history they contain as proof that she was founded by Christ himself and commissioned by him, and that she has ever been loyal to his teaching and his mission.

The gospels are translated and are constantly being translated anew into all the languages of the world. They are the subject of the prayer and meditation of thousands, of millions of people.

They were written in the first century of our Christian era, a long time ago, but they speak to us today as they have in every age since they were first written, to millions and millions of Christian hearts.

They have been praised as literature, as poetry, as history. They have been praised as character studies and for their masterful psychology. They have been studied and restudied as no other book before or since. Men have loved — and hated — them and their message and the Man they present to the world, with a fierceness, a violence, that seems incredible.

There is, in short, no need at all to justify taking a little more time and a little more paper and ink to do a little more thinking and writing about the gospels.

For their importance is evident. And, though there are many things that everyone knows about the gospels, there are still many, many things that everyone does not know. Perhaps there are even things that no one will ever know. But at least, as new knowledge does arise, and new insights are gained, it is worth while talking them over in public.

We have all heard from time to time that in recent years there has been much new truth discovered about the gospels. Improved scientific techniques of investigation, new discoveries about the historical background of the gospel times, have all contributed to this new knowledge. So has a new thirst for God's truth in an age which has more and more fully experienced the insufficiency of man's. To begin our own investigation into what some of this new material is and what it can tell us about the gospels we have always known and loved, it might be best to start with a few things that most of us do *not* know about the gospels, and with a few things about them that may perhaps have often caused us to wonder.

For example, in reading the gospels through, we notice that three of them at least, and to a certain extent all four, recount the same incidents from the life of Christ. Since they are telling the story of the same Person, this might not seem too odd at first. After all, we would expect different biographies of the same man to overlap. They would tell the same incidents from different points of view perhaps, but the incidents would be essentially the same, since after all there is nothing for a good biography to do but recount those events which did happen.

But then we reflect that the gospels are not by any means *complete* biographies. Four books which told everything possible about Jesus would of course have to overlap. But four "books" which average seventy or eighty pages apiece in a modern edition, and especially books of the gospel type, are something else again. Four different biographies of relatively brief scope which tried to recount one whole life in summary, general fashion, might well overlap more than they differed. But as we read the gospels, we see that they do not tell the life of Jesus in a summary general fashion. They tell his life mainly by recounting individual anecdotes concerning him: how he dealt with this sick person or that, how he answered a certain critic, how he told a certain story. But the same anecdotes, the same healings, fragments of conversations, and parables, keep coming up in one gospel after another. This can be seen at once in any copy of the New Testament which has cross references to the other gospels noted in the margins or at the bottom of the page.

Yet one of the gospels tells us that Jesus did and taught so many things "that, should they all be recorded in full detail, the world is not likely to hold all the volumes that would have to be written" (Jn 21, 25). And common sense tells us that a man who led the active public life that Jesus did for about three years, who made all the friends and the enemies he did, who stirred the crowds of thousands as he did, who healed — in the very words of the gospels — all who came to him, must have lived through hundreds, thousands of incidents like those few recorded in our written gospels. And we know that his first followers held that his every word, his every action, was a precious treasure to be preserved, remembered, and passed on.

Why then have just some forty-odd stories come down to us? Why have we been left just these four brief accounts, all of them together insufficient to make more than one very slim little

volume? And why is such a large part of each of the four accounts, practically speaking, a repetition of what is found in the
others? There is something strange here, something most people
do not know about the gospel.

Another point worth wondering about a bit is this: when we
study the gospels in school or read introductory works on them, we
often come across the statement that the gospels are the record of
the preaching of various apostles. For example, that the gospel of
Mark is the record of the preaching of St. Peter, that Luke records
the preaching traditions of St. Paul, that John and Matthew recount the preaching of those two apostles. Yet, when we reflect
upon these statements, is it really clear what they mean? What
kind of sermons might those have been? Did the apostles actually,
in preaching, just tell the story of the life of Christ? Did they
simply narrate what he did, what he said, how he went from this
place to that, ending with the story of his death and resurrection?
Or did they tell one or two of the shorter individual stories from
Christ's life in each sermon or instruction, much as we read a
selection from the gospels today at mass? And if so, did that story
alone suffice? Were there not lessons drawn from the stories,
morals pointed, applications made? And if there were, why does
the "record of the apostolic preaching" omit all that and give only
the stories themselves, on which the real sermons were based? Or
if they did not draw those lessons and make those applications in
their sermons and instructions, then must not the word "preaching"
have had a very different sense then from what it has now? But if
so, what was that sense?

Or again, along the same line, it is said that the gospels sum up
the apostolic teaching, at least in its main lines; that this is one
of the main reasons the Church has always been able to appeal
to the gospels in establishing her own teachings as the divine
revelation taught by Christ and the apostles. Yet it strikes us at
once how different the gospels are from any summary presentation
of Christian doctrine that a preacher or teacher would make today.
How many of us, if asked to write a brief account of what Christians believe, would come up with sixty pages that resembled

one of the gospels? Would we not present a doctrinal outline rather than a history? And would we not center our exposition around the Trinity, the Incarnation, the Church, the Sacraments?

All these things are at the center of revealed doctrine. That they are in the gospels is not to be doubted. But that they are its center, that these points are handled more than indirectly and in a scattered, disorganized fashion in the gospels, is, if true, certainly not immediately clear and evident to the modern reader. But if not, why not? In what sense is a gospel a summary of the apostolic preaching and teaching? Or perhaps we should ask, just what did the apostles preach and teach?

Again, there is a whole series of expressions in which the word "gospel" does not seem to mean one of the four written gospels we know. For example, Jesus said that his gospel, his good news, would be preached to many nations. "I assure you that wherever, in any part of the world, this gospel is preached, what this woman has just done will likewise be proclaimed to perpetuate her memory" (Mt 26, 13). Jesus, like John the Baptist before him, began his public career by announcing:

> "The time of waiting is over
> the kingdom of God is close at hand.
> Change your evil ways;
> believe in the gospel" (Mk 1, 15).

"Gospel" in such statements could hardly mean the fourfold life of Christ we call the four gospels today. They were not yet written, the principal events which they record had not yet taken place. What were the people then supposed to do in order to "believe the gospel"? We can search the recorded sayings of John the Baptist and of Jesus and we never find them clearly saying, "Here is the gospel. Here is the good news to which I referred. Believe this." Why not?

Or when St. Paul says, "according to my gospel" (Rom 2, 16), does he refer to a gospel according to Paul, to be ranked with the gospel according to Matthew and the rest? When he writes: "I am not ashamed of the gospel, for it is the power of God to all who believe" (Rom 1, 16), what gospel is he talking about? Some gospel, some good news, certainly, but precisely what good news? And how can it, the gospel, be "the power of God to all who believe"? Perhaps any instructed Christian should already know the answer. And yet it can do no harm to pose the question and see whether a further examination of scripture and tradition can help us formulate our answer a bit more clearly than we may have been able to do up to now.

There are many, many other problems, small and large, that one can wonder about in the gospels. Why, for instance, are there four of them instead of just one? What about all this fulfillment of Old Testament prophecies which are not so easy for us today to recognize as genuinely prophetic in the first place? What about the miracles, the demons, the so-called "mythology" that disconcerts so many moderns? What about the historical accuracy of the accounts, even when they seem to differ among themselves or contradict one another? To pose the classic instances: Did Christ heal one blind man at Jericho or two? Was it at the entrance to the city or as he left the city? Did he say at the last supper "This is my blood" (Matthew; Mark) or "This chalice is the new testament in my blood" (Luke; 1 Corinthians)? Must we conclude from the differing versions in our gospels that no one of the accounts aims at giving our Lord's exact words, even on so solemn an occasion and at a moment of such importance for the future life of the Church?

Questions about the gospels are not lacking. And today, in this modern age, neither are answers. Perhaps there are too many answers. The answers are often enough based upon different views of what the gospels are and what the evangelists are trying to do. In this book we are going to try an approach aimed above all at finding out what the basic gospel message was. And we are basing the approach on the most commonly held scholarly opinions of today as to what a gospel is and what an evangelist was trying to do. That he was trying to present the Christian message is clear. But exactly how? As a catechism? As a simple record of things which happened, from which each one would then be free to draw his own conclusions? As a mere unorganized collection of traditions and stories about Jesus, and writing down of such words of Jesus as happened still to be remembered? The point of view we take on these and similar questions will be very important in forming our conclusions.

We are trying to find in the gospels what Catholic tradition and dogma have always insisted is there; that is, above all, the word of God, God's revelation to us. In that sense this is a theology of the gospels. It is looking for meaning above all. It is looking for the Christian message.

Fortunately, in making this attempt, we have many helps that a writer of fifty years ago would not have had. For scientific criticism of the gospels in the past generation has advanced far beyond the crude materialistic approach that once gloried in the name of "rationalism." It was the fashion, not long ago, for all who wanted to be recognized as scientific in their gospel studies, to approach the gospel text with a set of presuppositions, which were supposed to keep their criticism objective, unwarped by sectarian religious prejudice. The intention was good. But its net effect was to rule out from the very first any breaking through of the supernatural into our real world.

Were miracles recorded? But miracles are impossible. Therefore the gospels are unhistorical, fictional. Is Christ treated as divine redeemer? But he was only a man. Therefore the gospels are myths. Why are these things impossible? Because they do not happen otherwise. Of course this overlooks the very point of writing the gospels in the first place: that something had occurred which had never happened before. And ultimately this led to a certain cast of mind where, more often than not, the very fact that some point or other was found in the Christian tradition concerning the gospels made it seem more likely that the opposite was true. Are the gospels traditionally ascribed to Matthew, Mark, Luke, and John? Then some scientific investigators were more ready to accept as their authors almost anyone who could be named or imagined rather than those venerable personages. Why? Simply to avoid prejudicing their own objectivity as scientific investigators.

Of course it eventually became obvious that this was only to let new prejudices take the place of the old, that ultimately this was not a scientific approach at all. Since then, the contrary realization has been growing that the gospels, like any other piece of literature, must be taken first of all for what they are. And they are religious writings, with religious aims and religious backgrounds. And as a consequence the most truly scientific interpretation is a sympathetic religious interpretation.

This does not mean, of course, that the scientific critic cannot read a religious document and study it without first accepting the faith for which it stands and from which it comes. That would mean that only Mohammedans could write works on the Koran, only Hindus on the Vedas. But it does mean that the best way to approach the Vedas is not to begin by asking whether or not they portray accurately and in detail the historical facts about ancient Indian methods of warfare. One must rather begin by accepting them as they stand and for what they claim to be, and try to grasp in their own terms what they are trying to say, what philosophic and religious message they are trying to convey.

Questions as to what historical facts lie *behind* these documents are interesting and important — for history. But they do not necessarily promote the literary understanding of the documents at all. This is true even though the religious message of the gospels is precisely the message that a certain something actually happened to real men in this real world. That fact tempts one to reach at once for the yardstick of historical criticism. But one must not reach too fast. The scientific critic today tries first to understand the document and the document's message in its own terms. Only as a second step, when he is sure of what the document is trying to say, when he feels he knows definitely to what sort of history the document is appealing, does he feel free to ask himself, in the case of the Vedas, what history really lies behind them, and in the case of the gospels whether their claims can be historically justified. This is a turnabout in modern criticism. Nineteenth-century critics should not have been surprised to find that the gospels were not written like nineteenth-century history books. But they were surprised. And they tried to reject the gospels on that account. Twentieth-century investigators try to avoid similar fatal errors.

An especially important development of the past fifty years has been the study of the growth of the gospels in the Church. We always knew that the gospels were written in the Church and by the Church. Even where eyewitness material is to be found in the gospels, it has never been commonly supposed that the eyewitnesses were jotting things down while they happened, or that the evangelists, like so many Boswells, conversed with Jesus, notebooks in hand.

It was always known that the gospels were written some time after the events that they recount — somewhere between twenty and seventy years afterward. The Church has always insisted on this fact as extremely important, for it proves that the gospels cannot possibly be quoted *against* the Church, they are completely her book, her own production, written in, by, and for her. The gospels and the rest of the New Testament do not and cannot stand over against the tradition of the Church. Rather they are a summing up of that very tradition. Nor do they constitute some higher court of appeal above tradition. They are the product of the Church's tradition. The oral teaching, the tradition of the Church, came first. The gospels and the New Testament followed after, a written recording of the truths which the tradition proclaimed, preserving fixed for all time a picture of that tradition as it flourished in the first and second Christian generations.

It is precisely this aspect of the production of the gospels which has gained tremendous prominence in modern scientific study of the gospels. The gospels did not drop ready-made from heaven. They were written in the Church. They record the tradition of the Church in regard to Christ. And, since they were written some years after the events they record, one can study in them something of that living tradition as it flourished in the years between our Lord's death and the writing of the gospels. One can find in them what the Church taught and preached about Jesus. One can even find in them how the Church of the first century applied the sayings and deeds of Jesus to the problems of her time.

To appreciate these gospels, a unique sort of record of a unique sort of events, we shall try to catch this oral tradition of the first generation on the fly, as it really was growing up between the time Christ ascended to his Father and the time the gospels were written. To do this we have to go outside the gospels themselves, but not outside the New Testament. For the Church has also preserved for us as scripture a record of that early history on the move, of that growth of tradition in the first generations, in the book of the Acts of the Apostles.

The book of Acts was written by St. Luke as a continuation of his own gospel. In it he traces the progress of the Church from the day Christ left his apostles for the last time up to the time of Paul's imprisonment at Rome, that is, from about the year 30 to about the year 60. It was a time of enormous development, of growing self-realization for the Church. It is the apostolic age, that is, precisely the age of the Church to which Christ had promised in a special way the instruction and illumination of the Holy Spirit, to teach them all things which they could not yet bear or understand while he was still with them.

St. Luke's book of Acts lets us see that developing consciousness of the Church. He lets us see her change from what was outwardly just one more small sect within Judaism, faithful to the temple observances of the Jews, to the dietary laws, to circumcision and all the rest, into a consciously world-oriented religion, engaged in an active and successful missionary program, and establishing itself firmly in the important centers of world activity of the day: in Antioch, Ephesus, Athens, Corinth, and finally in Rome.

As is typical of ancient histories, the story of Acts is told not so much in abstract, third-person summaries of events with lists of dates and names and places, but characteristically by means of a series of talks, discourses. From the religious nature of the subject matter being communicated, these discourses in Acts are for the most part what we would call sermons. That is, they have a religious nature and subject and purpose, and they are aimed at getting their hearers to take religious action, to believe in and follow Christ.

One of the most interesting things about these sermons in Acts is this: they present the subject matter, the basic truth about Jesus Christ, to different classes of hearers in what seems to be a deliberately ordered sequence, according to the general plan of the movement of the whole book. There is a sermon on Christ for the very first converts, all of them loyal Jews. There is another for the Jews who will reject the message, the same groups who sought Christ's death. There is a sermon for Gentiles, non-Jews, who have however been living among the Jewish people and have some familiarity with the background teachings of their laws and their scriptures. And there are sermons for non-Jews who have no idea at all of the one true God, and who have never heard of God's great promises to Israel.

These sermons are arranged in a progressive order of ever greater expansion, to correspond with Luke's basic outline of the Church moving outward from Jerusalem and encountering new and changing problems every step of the way. Her solutions to these problems and reactions to these trials as they occur show up in the text of the sermons.

At the same time, this tends to produce in the sermons an expanding, ever fuller explanation of what Christ was and did and what he means to the world. As we follow this line of expansion, we find ourselves coming to see and understand something of the process of growth of the four gospels. For Acts shows us the Church seeking and finding in all Christ has left her — with the aid of the inspiring, indwelling Holy Spirit — the answers to ever new questions as they arise, and it is this same Church which, toward the end of the period described in Acts, is going to be engaged in composing the canonical gospels. The gospels will bear the mark of what she has learned in the Spirit about Christ's message and meaning for the world. The gospels will be her fuller, more adequate account to the world of what Christ is and of what he taught and what he demands of every man.

At this point, a difficulty may well be raised: is not the book of Acts a religious book with a religious message, just as the gospels are? With what right then can we here use it much as we might a page from an ordinary history book in order to find out what lies behind the gospel story, to find out how the gospels came to be written and what they mean?

The point is well taken. And as a matter of fact, it is true that such a procedure would be to make a prejudiced approach much like the one we were criticizing just a few pages earlier. But that is not what we are doing. For the basis for this present analytic-historical use of the book of the Acts is not the book as a finished product, the way it came from the pen of St. Luke. As a finished product, it was and is above all a religious document, and falls into a special class of literature all its own, closer perhaps to the gospel form than to a modern history text. Our analysis, however, is based not on that finished work, but on the individual sermons which are included in it. And the interesting and curious thing is this: it is not by a mere literary device of the author of Acts that those sermons represent an ever expanding point of view and an ever surer theological self-grasp in the early Church. Nor is it the late first-century theology of the author which they mirror. Judging from internal evidences of vocabulary and style, as well as from comparisons with other contemporary literature, critical historians today generally agree that those sermons have been, for the most part, actually preserved from approximately the time when each of them was actually delivered. How, why, in what language, we do not know. But the historical evidence is all in favor of their actually reflecting the developing thought of the first-century Church.

All in all then, these sermons are among the most important material available for a study of our written gospels and for an attempt to determine just what the writers of the gospels thought they were doing, what aim they had in mind, and exactly what presuppositions they were looking for in their audiences and hearers.

But we shall not stop there. We have other firsthand documents which give us the teaching of the Church face to face with the problems of that first age. These are the letters of St. Paul and of other writers of the first generation, preserved for us in the epistles of the New Testament. With the clues gained from the sermons in Acts, we have some idea of what to look for in these writings in our attempts to dig out the fundamental gospel message. We will try then to see how the most frequently and constantly recurring themes of these letters fit into the basic outline of the apostolic preaching. With their help, we shall see filled out the message and teaching which we find fixed at last in our four gospels.

This is all too vague as stated so far. But it should take on flesh and life as we progress in our study through the next few chapters. Then we shall apply all we have learned in this way to the gospels as we possess them, and finally see what light all this together sheds on the constant traditional life and teaching of the Church, thus finishing, let us hope, with a fuller and deeper grasp of just what is this good news.

CHAPTER 2

Good News for Israel: The Promises Are Fulfilled

THE first time the apostles announced the gospel message to the world was on the first Christian Pentecost. The story is told in the second chapter of the Acts of the Apostles. Here is the sermon Peter preached:

"... this [which you see] is what was foretold by the prophet Joel:

'It shall happen in the last days, says God,
that I will pour forth my Spirit on all mankind;
And your sons and daughters shall prophesy,
and your young men shall see visions,
and your old men shall dream dreams.
And on my slaves too and my handmaids
in those days will I pour forth my Spirit,
and they shall prophesy.
I will also show wonders in the heavens above
and signs on the earth below,
blood and fire and a cloud of smoke.
The sun shall be turned into darkness
and the moon into blood,
Before the day of the Lord comes,
the great and manifest day.
And it shall happen
that whoever calls on the name of the Lord
shall be saved.'

"Men of Israel, hear these words. Jesus of Nazareth was a man accredited to you by God through miracles and wonders and

16

signs, which God did through him in your midst, as you yourselves know. When he was delivered up by the settled purpose
and foreknowledge of God, you crucified and slew him by the
hands of wicked men. But God has raised him up, having put an
end to the pangs of death, because it was not possible that death
should hold him. For David says of him:

'I saw the Lord before me always,
because he is at my right hand lest I be stricken.
This is why my heart has made merry
and my tongue has rejoiced.
Even my flesh will rest in hope,
because you will not abandon my soul to death
and you will not let your Holy One see decay.
You have made known to me the path that leads to life;
You will fill me with joy in your presence.'

"Brothers, we are permitted to speak with firm assurance to
you of the patriarch David that he died and was buried. His
tomb is with us to this day. Therefore, since he was a prophet
and knew that God had sworn to him with an oath that of his
offspring one was to sit on his throne, he spoke with foreknowledge of the resurrection of the Christ, who was not
abandoned to the grave and whose flesh did not see decay.
God has raised up this Jesus, and of that fact we are all witnesses. Therefore, exalted by the power of God, and receiving
from the Father the promised Holy Spirit, he has poured forth
that which you see and hear. David did not ascend into heaven,
but he says:

'The Lord said to my Lord,
Sit at my right hand,
until I make your enemies
a footstool for your feet."

"Therefore, let all Israel know most assuredly that God has
made him both Lord and Christ — this very Jesus whom you
have crucified."

On hearing this they were pierced to the heart and said to
Peter and the rest of the apostles, "Brothers, what shall we do?"

"Have a change of heart and mind," Peter told them, "and be
baptized everyone of you in the name of Jesus Christ for the
remission of your sins: then you will receive the gift of the
Holy Spirit. The promise is meant for you and for your children
and for all who are afar off, for all whom the Lord our God may
call to himself" (Acts 2, 16–39).

The sermon is recorded only in outline. But even on the day the whole talk was first delivered it was not directed to twentieth-century hearers. There is nothing surprising then in the fact that it does not produce an immediate and clear effect on us today as it stands. It is directed to Jewish listeners of another age, who lived and acted, thought and prayed against a cultural background very different from our own. The sermon did successfully answer to their background and to their needs and expectations. Resoundingly so. For "there were added that day (to the Church) some three thousand persons" (Acts 2, 41). A highly effective sermon.

To make the point of it clearer to ourselves, we will have to study it more deeply. First of all then, those "promises to the fathers," those "predictions of the prophets" — to show that these are being fulfilled seems to be Peter's first concern. We shall find the same emphasis every time we look at a New Testament sermon to a Jewish audience. What are these promises and predictions? What was in the mind of the listening Jewish audience when they heard the preachers refer to these things? The speakers are obviously taking for granted that their hearers do understand. The results show that they did. But for those of us who have perhaps not prayed and sung and listened to the Old Testament every day of our lives as they had, who have not wept over the prophets' laments or thrilled to their dreams of the future as we know they did, for us there may remain some questions to be answered. What promises are these preachers talking about? And how have they been fulfilled in what has happened to Jesus of Nazareth? And why was this such good news?

God's promises to the Jewish people run all through the Old Testament. They were, one might almost say — or at least they had become — the very reason for existence to the Jewish people. The promises began as far back as Abraham, first father of the Jews, if not actually even earlier, with Adam, Seth, Noah. God had promised, as recorded in the sacred writings of the Jews, that he would make Abraham and his descendants into a great nation. He had promised to give them the land of Canaan for their possession forever. He had promised to David and his successors dominion over the land forever, a royal and eternal kingship in one unbroken line. He had promised the Israelites victory and triumph over their enemies. He had promised a future when all the world would look to Israel as leader, as teacher, as guide, when the nations would stream to Mount Sion to adore, to learn, to seek out Israel's God. He had promised that he would be Israel's God forever, dwelling in their midst, keeping them safe, providing for all their needs. He had promised moreover symbolically, in the old-time acts of favor and protections he had worked, that he would continue to be to them a savior, a refuge, and a shield in all their trials as he had been then. He had foretold that the mighty empires of the earth which had afflicted Israel would, one after the other, pass away and perish forever.

And then, through the prophets, more and more insistently, he had foretold a future day when all evil and evildoers in all the world together would be judged, crushed, done away with, purged out, destroyed. A day when all the good would be brought to everlasting peace by their God. A day when the wrongs of the earth would be righted, when wars and suffering, hunger and thirst, oppression and cruelty would all be done away with forever.

And he had foretold, though still more obscurely, a future ONE who would be his perfect instrument for the accomplishment of all this. A prince of the line of David, a priest of the order of Melchizedek, a servant, especially anointed as God's own chosen one to do God's special work, a conqueror, a king, a suffering one, a lamb, a great prophet, a preacher of good news.

All this, in brief, God had promised Israel. We find it laid out for us in the pages of the Old Testament. The promises strike us as being of many different orders and types at once. They are physical and literal, they are metaphorical and idealistic. They are corporeal, they are spiritual. They seem to be catering to man's lower instincts — his desire for vengeance on his enemies for example — as well as to his highest and noblest dreams. They promise things that later generations could clearly see had been actually granted and obtained, as the possession of the land of Israel, the collapse and destruction of Babylon, Edom, Assyria. They promised things not yet attained, but at least imaginable to the Jews of that time (however improbable in a literal sense they strike us as being today): the final physical defeat of the enemies who remained, the exaltation of Israel — tiny Israel — to world leader and teacher. And they promised finally things that were just barely imaginable by anyone — things whose realization would demand almost that God create an entirely new human type altogether; that is, such things as the reign of perfect and universal peace and justice (with its accompanying changes in the order of nature itself, when the lion should lie down with the lamb). Finally they promised things which could perhaps be accomplished by an overwhelming intervention of God into history, but certainly only thus; such things as the complete and utter conquest, judgment, and definitive extermination of all the wicked, and the perfect triumph and justification before all the world of those who had been faithful and just.

These were, in general and brief outline, the things to which the Jews could rightly look forward as having been promised. And look forward to them they did. This never dying hope in the future sustained them time and time again in the most severe trials. To this hope the prophets pointed, of this the people dreamed. This sustained them in exile, in persecution, in oppression. In the books of Esther, in Daniel, Maccabees, in all the accounts of the afflictions of the people, in exile, in oppression, the same cries rise up over and over: "Thou hast promised, thou hast promised. As you spoke once to Moses, to David, fulfill your word. Save us as thou hast promised." And God's word comes back through his prophets again and again: "I will be faithful to that which I have spoken." As the epistle to the Hebrews sums it up, after listing many of the classic exploits of the people, accomplished by their faith in the promises of God:

And what more shall I say? Time would fail me to tell of Gedeon, Barac, Samson, Jepthe, David, and Samuel, and the prophets, who by faith conquered kingdoms, enforced justice, had promises realized, stopped the mouths of lions, put out raging fires, escaped the edge of the sword, became strong when they were weak, grew valiant in battle, routed invading armies. Women recovered their dead children brought back to life. Others in the hope of rising to a better life were beaten to death rather than accept release. Others endured bitter mockery and scourging, yes, even chains and imprisonment. They were stoned, they were sawed asunder, they were put to death by the sword. They went from place to place, clothed in sheepskins and goat-skins, destitute, distressed, mistreated. The world was not worthy of them. They wandered about seeking refuge in deserts, hills, caves, and holes in the ground. All these, to whom their faith had borne favorable testimony, did not receive the promised blessings, because God, holding better blessings in reserve for us, would not have them reach perfection apart from us (Heb 11, 32–40).

And just how were all these promises interpreted at the precise time at which Christ and the apostles preached? Just what were those Jews of the early first century of the Christian era thinking, believing, hoping? To what promises did they look forward? To the same ones as had their fathers? And what method of fulfillment did they hope for and expect? What delivery did they expect God to work? What did the promises mean to Christ's contemporaries?

To find this out we have to consult the evidence of the writings composed at that time and immediately before it. From one large body of such writing, the so-called apocalyptic literature, we get the impression that they laid special stress at this period on the great and final consummation of all things, the end of the world, which God was to work suddenly, swiftly, and powerfully. This was seen as automatically exalting Israel, for God was considered in the apocalyptic literature as identifying his own rise and fall, success and failure, with that of the people of Israel. This same great and final deed would be also automatically the exaltation of the just — again identified practically with Israel, the only people faithful to God's law.

Note that we are describing only the point of view of the apocalyptic literature. That this is a false point of view, or at least that this is not by any means an adequate picture of what the Old Testament itself teaches, we shall see later. But this is what the writers of these apocalypses — which were not inspired books, not a part of Sacred Scripture — really believed, and it is clear that this belief must have reflected a certain rather widespread sentiment in Israel.

However, other parties in Israel held a different view. They stressed another aspect of the promises. These looked to the exaltation of the nation, the smiting of its enemies, as the main thing to come. They looked forward to a holy war, a crusade, against the oppressors of Israel — which at this particular time meant above all the Romans. They would fight this war, they thought, as the Maccabees had fought theirs, under God's guidance, with God's help; but the millennium which lay ahead they seemed to see as something to be forged more by their own strong fighting hand than by a miraculous divine intervention.

Evidence of the existence of both these groups has been found at Qumran, among the now famous Dead Sea Scrolls. So have indications that the hope for the fulfillment of promises may have taken many other forms in practice. This is easy to understand. The scriptural phrasing of the promises is, as we saw, highly diversified. The many different elements it presents are not easy to synthesize and integrate. It is a natural human tendency in such a case to seize on one side of a thing or the other, and let the rest go.

Some of the Qumran texts seem to place emphasis above all on the new Israel of the "remnant." They bring out the prophetic doctrine that God was specially calling a select few among the people to help bring the promised new age into being by their own special faithfulness to the law. These looked forward, it seems, to an individual Messiah and teacher, a Messiah of Aaron (and?) a Messiah of Judah.

Our own gospels tell us of still other expectations among the people about such a personal agent of the Almighty, sent by God, anointed by him to rule and guide Israel, to shepherd his flock. This is the thinking behind such questions as: "Art thou he that is to come?" "Art thou the anointed one, the Christ? Art thou Elias? Moses?" Such people were "looking for the redemption of Jerusalem" and "the coming of the Lord's Christ."

Were there then none who interpreted God's promises to Israel in what would today be considered a strictly "religious" way? Did all think somehow in terms of national glory? Did no one see that there was a justice besides being a son of the law? Probably not. At least, the very posing of these questions, the attempt to make such distinctions, takes us out of the usual Old Testament categories and ways of thinking and into our own. And therefore it almost certainly takes us away from the way of thinking of that first-century audience too. This was justice as God had taught it to them: life in Israel. And Israel was God's people. Loyalty to God which was not loyalty to the nation simply made no sense. And a divine redemption, a divine promise, which was not somehow a promise to the people for their redemption would not have made much sense either. And so in their apocalyptic thinking, in their reading of the prophecies and promises, there is no question that welfare of people and state and religion and justice and God were all inextricably mixed up together, were one reality for them. And God's coming salvation would save them all together.

Now, historically, into the midst of all this, Christ came. The evangelists show how he let himself be identified with the Jewish hopes for the future; how, in fact, he encouraged this identification — without, however, personally making too explicit what shape exactly the promised future was to have.

He was called and let himself be called the Holy One of God, the Christ, the Messiah, the Son of David, the Son of God. The hopes he was arousing, stimulating, and answering are indicated in remarks and questions like: "Wilt thou at this time restore the kingdom to Israel?" "The Lord God will give him the throne of David his father. He will reign in the house of Jacob forever." "The Lord has anointed me. . . ." "Art thou he who is to come or shall we look for another?" "The blind see, the lame walk, the poor have the gospel preached to them." " 'If thou art the Christ, tell us plainly. . . . Art thou the Christ, the Son of the living God?' 'Thou sayest it. And I say, you will see the Son of Man coming upon the clouds of heaven. . . .' "

Jesus spoke of this future often as "the kingdom of God." He delivered once or twice what certainly seems to us a thorough-going apocalyptic discourse. He must have been fully conscious of the images these things were likely to evoke in the minds of his listeners. But for him they were only steps in a total program. Above all and in all, in his appeal to classic Messianic titles, in his demand for personal faith in himself, he was focusing attention and emphasis on himself, on his own person, as the center of religion and of life. And that was the important thing. In that sense, with that aim, he let himself be known and thought of as the embodi-ment of Israel's hopes.

The apostles themselves exemplify these expectations about Jesus. After his death, two of them leaving Jerusalem tell a stranger on the way: "We had hoped that he might be the man destined to redeem Israel" (Lk 24, 21). It is obvious that this hope had nothing to do with suffering and dying. It was redemption in the traditional biblical sense of snatching out from the hands of enemies, of delivering from oppression, which they had hoped for. It was his suffering and dying which now left them so disappointed. While he was still alive with them they had called him Master, Lord, and asked: "Give us a seat, one at your right, the other at your left, in your glory" (Mk 10, 37). "They disputed among themselves which should be the greatest" (Mk 9, 34). "Lord, when shall these things be?" (Mk 13, 4.)

Not that hints are at all lacking in Jesus' recorded words to show that his conception of the destiny of Israel and the kingdom which was to come differed from that of the apostles: "You do not realize what you are asking. Can you drink the cup that I am to drink?" (Mk 10, 38). "Not everyone that says to me, 'Lord, Lord,' shall enter into the kingdom of heaven, but only he that does the will of my Father who is in heaven" (Mt 7, 21). "The Son of Man did not come into the world to be served but to serve and to give his life as a ransom for many" (Mk 10, 45).

Still, all that Jesus said in this direction apparently never quite penetrated their minds. And if it was never understood by the apostles, we may be sure it was much less understood by the multitudes. Up to the very moment of our Lord's ascension, the apostles are still looking for the bringing in of the kingdom to Israel. And as late as that, he still does not disillusion them. He does not say, "Dear thick-headed ones, please finally understand. There is not going to be any kingdom of Israel. I'm talking about a spiritual kingdom, a Church, and about God's rule in souls, and about eternal happiness in the next life, after death."

Jesus never said this, so far as we know. It would have been easy to do, we tend to think. What reason had he to feel so disillusioned and unhappy over their constant misunderstandings if he never spelled the truth out for them? But even at this last moment, he does not answer "There is not going to be any kingdom of the kind you think." Instead he says only, "It is not for you to know the times or the dates that the Father has fixed by his own authority" (Acts 1, 7). He does not really enlighten them, but only tells them they must wait a bit.

Christ was then the hope of Israel for all who believed and followed him in the same undefined sense that the promises themselves expressed this hope. In general the promises stood for "all good things" for the people of God, the answer to every dream, the perfection and fulfillment of every wish. So too did Jesus. This is what the people saw in Jesus, and what they were given foretastes of in his cures and in the drawing power of his extraordinary personality. When they dealt with him, heard him, looked at him, listened to his words, all was hope for the future. As they believed in him, the whole future came to depend on him, all good to be embodied in him. Of course not all believed that God's salvation was to come through a single man. And not all could accept the idea that it might come through a man like Jesus. Those Israelites who were committed to another view of what God's salvation was to be, who refused to see that it could be embodied in this man, naturally opposed him violently. Those who, for example, saw Israel's hope in war and rebellion, in politics, in legalistic fulfillment, in themselves, would detach themselves from Jesus and even attack him in the measure in which they saw he was not acting in accord with their own plans and notions, just as they would and did attack him and hate him in the measure in which they saw that his success (or failure, or even continued existence) could be a threat to their own favored scheme for Israel's salvation.

In his close disciples, on the other hand, all we have said of the general hopes of the people would be found still more intensely. They above all were really staking everything on him and on what they believed was his certain, divinely foreordained success.

Still, even among these disciples, we cannot be sure in detail and with exactness just what they expected of him. To some extent this would have varied from man to man. Perhaps they would not have been too certain themselves, if asked, how to spell it out in any detail. What does a man hope for from the new job he takes, the wife he marries, the president he votes for? So in their case, they had some ideas of a better future, some notion of an ideal they wanted or vaguely dreamed of, and they knew only that it was to come about in and through Jesus. He had said, "Come follow me." They had not asked questions; they had simply come.

His arrest, trial, crucifixion, and death changed all that, destroyed it at one blast. One moment it was there, it was everything, it was their whole lives. The next moment it simply did not exist. Everything was gone. Everything was wrong. Christ was dead. The world was empty. And heaven seemed empty too. There were no hopes for Israel. Not in this Christ at any rate. He was dead. They had seen him die. They had laid him in a tomb. Could they now shift over to some other party, could they find tomorrow some other hoped-for embodiment of God's promises, the promises which they had now become so thoroughly accustomed to understanding and thinking about only in terms of Jesus? Promises which they had even explained to others in his name as Israel's whole hope for the future? Could they now go back to being pharisees? Zealots? Nothing? Would they give up all hope?

That they thought of all this explicitly and in just this way is not too probable either. Probably all they could think and feel with any clearness was ache and emptiness and shock. Of meaning and purpose and design they could find none. How should they? It was over. He was dead.

It is so easy for us nowadays to criticize their attitude, to say, well, after all, Jesus had foretold his suffering and death. So easy to say, so psychologically obtuse. Perhaps the fact that he had foretold suffering and death for himself and them did ease the shock a bit. Perhaps. But the main fact is: on this man they had staked all they had and hoped for, and here he lay before them, dead. This man was to have saved Israel. And he could not, did not, save himself from the cross. They had, some of them, stood and seen it happen. Christ had failed — if this man was the Christ. But no, the Christ could not fail, not the real Christ. But who then was this their Lord? Those were empty, hard days.

We must actually meditate long and carefully on this loss, this frustration of the promises in the minds of the disciples if we are to understand what happened next and what they finally came to see in the promises.

For again, and of a sudden, everything changed. Christ was not lost, Christ had not failed. He was risen from the dead. They saw him, they spoke with him, they ate and drank with him, they received new instruction again from his mouth. With his help and the help of the Holy Spirit which he now gave them, they took another look at the prophecies and promises. They looked at them now in the light of what had happened to Jesus, in the light of his death and resurrection. And they saw the old promises suddenly transformed before their eyes, turned inside out almost — and as a result making perfect and complete sense for the first time. We shall study this more in detail in Chapter 11.

The promises, then, to which Peter refers in his speech, are that David, in the person of one of his descendants, will not taste corruption; that a descendant of David will be the Messiah in whom all good things will be granted to Israel; that when the Messianic age does come God's Spirit will be poured forth upon all who call upon the name of the Lord. Peter says that Jesus is that descendant of David who has not tasted corruption, whose soul has not been left in the land of the dead, but whom God has raised from the tomb. Jesus is then the Messiah foretold in whom all good things will come to Israel. And therefore the Messiah is here, and the Messianic age is at hand.

And indeed, as Peter spoke, his hearers had evidence before their eyes that the Messianic age had truly begun. That is what had drawn the large crowd to come to hear him that day: the manifestations of the presence of God's Spirit in the whole apostolic group as described in the second chapter of Acts. The Spirit with his gifts and powers was being poured forth that first Christian Pentecost day on those who called upon the name of the Lord — that is, on those who believed that Jesus the crucified had been exalted to be Lord.

Peter is preaching then that one great promise has been fulfilled: their Messiah was indeed not left subject to death. One great promise was being fulfilled before their eyes: God's Spirit was descending upon men, upon all who called on the name of the Lord. The new age has dawned: from what has happened and from what is happening now, all the rest of God's blessings are about to flow onto Israel. The Jesus whom they had rejected and crucified is Lord and is Christ.

"On hearing this they were pierced to the heart and said to Peter and the rest of the apostles, 'Brothers, what shall we do?'" (Acts 2, 37.)

And now Peter explains that there *is* something for them to do if they are to enter into the promises. And the main thing is precisely to accept the shocking, the bizarre fact he had just told them: that the one they knew to have been rejected, condemned, and crucified was really God's chosen instrument of salvation, that the dead Jesus was now the risen Lord, that the discredited prophet was truly God's Messiah, his Christ.

What they must do is correct their notion of what the Messiah is and of God's plan for saving Israel. They must accept the fact that if God foretold that the Christ would rise, then God must have planned too that the Christ should die. They must face the fact that their longed-for Savior, Messiah, fulfillment of the promises and of their hopes, is in this man whom they had driven to the cross. And finally, they were being called to acknowledge and believe that this combination of dying and rising, as they now knew it in Jesus, was really their promised salvation. How it was, why it was, what connection it was to have with the future good things in store for them, they might not yet understand. But the fact was clear. The presence and working of the Spirit made it clear.

Could they then change their whole attitude and set of judgments that completely? Could they call upon him as Lord, him whom they had seen in disgrace, failure, death? Could they accept a baptism in his name — a public act of self-commitment to him and to the group which represented him in Israel? If so, they could experience this same gift of God which they saw working in the apostles and share in all that gift implied for the future:

> "Have a change of heart and mind . . . and be baptized everyone of you in the name of Jesus Christ for the remission of your sins: then you will receive the gift of the Holy Spirit. The promise is meant for you and for your children, and for all who are afar off, for all whom the Lord our God may call to himself" (Acts 2, 38–39).

The promise Peter refers to explicitly is the Spirit — according to the prophecy of Joel. All the rest that they had dreamed of is by no means denied. It is supposed as coming with the Spirit in the Messianic age of the Spirit which is now coming in. It comes in by their turning to the Messiah and being baptized in his name — for the taking away of sin. This last point they would recognize as the normal and expected prelude to any great act of God: the people entering on the Messianic promises must be especially holy and pure.

❋   ❋   ❋

Peter's second sermon is reported in Chapter 3 of Acts. The occasion was a new manifestation of the power of the Spirit and the power of faith in Jesus. Peter heals with a word a man who had been crippled from birth. His sermon is an explanation:

> "Why do you marvel at this man, or why do you stare at us, as though by any power or holiness of our own we had enabled him to walk? The God of Abraham, of Isaac, and of

Jacob, the God of our fathers, has glorified his servant, Jesus,
whom you indeed delivered up and disowned in the presence
of Pilate, when he had decided to release him. You, however,
disowned the Holy and Just One, and asked that a murderer
be released to you; but you killed the leader of life, whom
God has raised up from the dead. Of this fact we are witnesses.
And his name, that is when this man had faith in it, has made
him strong whom you behold and recognize. Moreover, it is
the faith that comes through Jesus that has given him this
perfect health in the presence of all of you" (Acts 3, 12–16).

The manifestation of the Spirit on Pentecost had been one
taste of the new age. This miraculous healing of the lame man
was another. Faith in the name of Jesus was what had brought
about both. Therefore Peter calls on his hearers to believe in
Jesus; that is, as we saw before, to accept the crucified one as
God's chosen, their Messiah, their Lord.

Peter finally makes explicit one additional point, not clear perhaps from the first sermon: that when all turn to acceptance of
this Christ, then sin and evil will finally be destroyed, then the
Christ will come again from heaven for the final restoration of
all things.

"Now brothers, I know that you acted in ignorance, as did
also your rulers. But in this way God fulfilled what he had
announced through all the prophets: that his Christ should
suffer. Have a change of heart, therefore; be converted, that
your sins may be blotted out, in order that so the times of
refreshment may come from the presence of the Lord, and
that he may send him who has been destined beforehand for
you as the Christ, Jesus. Heaven must receive him until the
times of the restoration of all things, of which God has spoken
through his holy prophets of old. . . . Now all the prophets
from Samuel onward, as many as have spoken, have also announced these days. You are the heirs of the prophets and of
the covenant that God made with your fathers, when he said
to Abraham,

'In your offspring shall
　all the families of the earth be blessed' "
(Acts 3, 17–25).

He closes the talk by reminding them once more how they are to inherit these promised blessings: by turning in faith and repentance to this Messiah, God's Messiah, the only Messiah there is, the crucified and risen Jesus: "To you first, God, having raised up his servant, has sent him to bless you, by turning everyone of you away from his own wickedness" (Acts 3, 26).

*　　*　　*

So in this first preaching to the Jews, the content of the promises remains unspecified in its details, except for their starting point — the gift of the Spirit and the marvelous works which result from it before their eyes. The effects this will produce on the nation are left as they were in the Old Testament and in Jewish extrabiblical tradition. That the promises have begun to arrive is the main point. The Messiah has come, Jesus. His own resurrection is the first act of the beginning new age. His sending of the Holy Spirit on them is the second. And now continued manifestations of the Spirit and of God's power will be the more and more frequently repeated signs of what is coming over the world, the age foretold by the prophets.

This is the good news as the apostles first spoke it and as it was first heard among the Jews. For its fuller meaning, a fuller explanation of the goodness in it, some account of how it was to change the history of Israel and Israel's understanding of God's action in history, we must wait until later chapters.

CHAPTER 3

Good News for the Nations: Christ Is Our Salvation

CHRIST'S message and Christ's salvation were not for the Jews alone, but for the entire world. We know that now. But it would not have been so easy to recognize that truth, listening to the first preaching of the little apostolic community at Jerusalem. The very approach to Christ as the fulfillment of God's promises tended to limit their view. The promises were to Israel. They had always been to Israel. They pointed forward to Israel's exaltation over the nations. They concerned the rest of the nations of the earth only insofar as all these others could and would, in subjection to Israel, or by becoming members of Israel themselves, share in the same benefits.

The apostles and all the other first Christians had been raised in this point of view from childhood. They could hardly conceive any other. Their attitude had nothing to do with a positive reprobation of the Gentiles to eternal perdition; nothing to do either with questions of segregation or prejudice. It was simply that they had been raised in a consciousness of their special relation as Israelites to Israel's God, an appreciation of God's closeness and direct dealings with themselves as a people; and that all this, as far as they had learned, had nothing directly to do with the Gentile world.

Israel's work was to honor God's name and to keep God's law. And this law was an expression of the special and personal covenant, pact, treaty, which God had made with the people of Israel.

One could not really, meaningfully keep the law without being born into or entering of one's own free will into the covenant with God and into that people. Not that anything else was forbidden, but simply that nothing else really made sense.

But we know that Christ's message was for the entire world, not for the Jews alone. And one of the hardest things for us to understand and accept as we read the New Testament is that apparently for the first several years after the death, resurrection, and ascension of Jesus, years in which they preached the good news of the fulfillment in Christ of all the promises to Israel, the Christians acted as if they did not know.

They considered themselves Jews in the fullest sense. God had, in Jesus, finally fulfilled his promises to the Jewish people. He had promised that "a remnant would be saved," a remnant through and in which the whole people would find salvation. They were that remnant.

But they show no consciousness of being called themselves to inaugurate a new external religious order by any action of their own. They feel no need to make a radical break with the old dispensation. They pray with the rest of the people in the temple, meet in the synagogues, observe the dietary and purity laws of the Old Testament, and all the rest. Christ, they knew, was the fulfillment of the law. But that he was also more, and that they themselves had already implicitly accepted him as more, and that he himself had given them teaching and done things to and for them which could no longer be contained in the old wine-skins of the Jewish religion — of all that for the first several years they show no clear consciousness at all in the records we possess.

"They were regular in their visits to the temple, praising and blessing God" (Lk 24, 53).

"Daily with one accord they attended the temple . . . " (Acts 2, 46).

"As Peter and John were going up to the temple at three o'clock in the afternoon, the hour of prayer . . . " (Acts 3, 1).

And when it is time to begin the mission to the Gentiles, it takes a special vision and revelation from God to make Peter realize it. In Acts 10 God shows him all manner of beasts, reptiles, and birds, and says: "Rise, Peter, kill and eat." But Peter, mindful of God's law in the Old Testament, says: "Never did I eat anything common or unclean." "What God has cleansed, do not call common!" And the Spirit tells him to go to the house of a certain Cornelius, a Roman military officer who is eager to speak with him. As Peter enters the house he says: "You know it is not permissible for a Jew to associate with a foreigner or to visit him, but God has shown me that I should not call any man common or unclean."

Nevertheless, in the following chapter, Chapter 11, we read: "Now the apostles and brothers all over Jerusalem heard that the Gentiles too had received God's word. When Peter went up to Jerusalem, those of the circumcision found fault with him, saying, 'You have visited and even eaten with uncircumcised men.'" But Peter proved to them that what he had done had God's approval, and "on hearing this, they acquiesced and glorified God, saying, 'Therefore to the Gentiles too God has given a change of heart and mind leading to life.'"

By the time this occurs, Acts has already recounted the first idyllic days of the Church at Jerusalem, the gradual conversion of many of the Jews, even of the Jewish priests (Chaps. 4 to 6). The story of the strife between "the Hebrews and the Hellenists" has already been told, the appointment of the seven deacons, the career and martyrdom of St. Stephen (Chaps. 6 and 7). This comes after the persecution at Jerusalem which followed Stephen's death and after the scattering of the disciples throughout Judea and Samaria. It is even later than the trip of Peter and John into Samaria after the persecution, when they went to check on and strengthen the communities which in the meantime had been founded there (Chap. 8). Saul had already done his persecuting and been stricken down on the road to Damascus. And now the Church was again at peace throughout all this district of Judea, Galilee, Samaria (9, 31). In other words, though we have no exact date for the incident, it is evident that at least several years had passed since Jesus left them before they were ready to make this first step toward preaching to Gentiles who did not observe the Law of Moses, and even then they needed a special revelation to assure them it was all right.

We ask ourselves: What about Christ's clear words in the gospels: "Go, therefore, and make all nations your disciples" (Mt 28, 19); "Preach the gospel to all creation . . . " (Mk 16, 15). "Wherever this gospel is preached in the whole world . . . " (Mt 26, 13)? We forget how many times in the course of the gospel narrative we find the comment, "They did not understand what he was saying to them" (Mk 9, 32).

It was Christ's will and authentic teaching that all men were to benefit from his words and work; but he also taught that after he was gone the Holy Spirit "will teach you everything, and refresh your memory of everything I have told you" (Jn 14, 26). This would be one instance of the fulfillment of this promise. The Holy Spirit did bring to their minds the full teaching of what Christ had taught and meant about the salvation of the Gentiles, but he did so only at the most opportune time, the time most favorable for leading them into a fuller understanding of the central message itself.

Only then did the real meaning of Christ's words open before their eyes, the full implications of stories like the Good Samaritan ("And who is my neighbor?"), or "crowds of people will arrive from east and from west and, in the company of Abraham, Isaac, and Jacob, will recline at table in the kingdom of heaven, when, at the same time, the born citizens of the realm will be hurled into the outer darkness" (Mt 8, 11–12). And "The Kingdom of God will be taken away from you and turned over to a nation that will produce the fruits expected of it" (Mt 21, 43). So too the story of the wedding feast, and the master who invited in the folk from the highways and byways when the originally invited showed no interest in coming to share his banquet. These and similar stories and sayings would all become clear in time.

After the conversion of the Roman centurion Cornelius, Acts tells us of the conversion of non-Jews at the Syrian city of Antioch, "and it was in Antioch that the disciples were first called

'Christians'" (Acts 11, 26). From then on the Church could be recognized even externally as more than just another Jewish sect with its own peculiar ideas about the Messiah. And from then on the importance and necessity of preaching to the Gentiles as well as the Jews was definitely accepted. Disputes, however, continued within the Church on the question of how fully the Gentile converts should be bound to observe the Mosaic Law. Toward the year 50 the Council of Jerusalem is discussing the question. And certainly in the heart and center of Judaism itself, the holy city of Jerusalem, the Christians continue to fulfill all the requirements of the ancient religion and law. As late as A.D. 58 Paul is greeted by St. James and the elders of the Church in Jerusalem with the words: "You see, brother, how many thousands of believers there are among the Jews, all of them zealous upholders of the Law. Now they have heard about you that you teach the Jews who live among the Gentiles to depart from Moses, advising them that they should not circumcise their children or observe the customs." And they give Paul directions as to what ceremonies he can perform so that "everybody will know that what they have heard about you is false, but that you too in your actions observe the Law" (Acts 21, 20 ff.). Reflecting on all this, we see how sensational a move it was to extend the preaching of the good news beyond the borders of Israel. We see what a revolution in the thinking of the leaders of the early Church that move must have demanded.

And what, in the first place, did God want the Gentiles to hear? How should they phrase the message? It was obvious that they could not simply preach to the Gentiles that the promises to Israel were fulfilled. They had to find other terms to express their message, terms the non-Jews would find meaningful. The message would continue to center on the fact of Christ's death and resurrection, but it would have to vary to meet the needs of their hearers. As they thought through the answer to this problem, they were destined to come, under the Holy Spirit, to a fuller and deeper understanding of what really had been meant all along by God's message and promises to the Jews.

They were faced from the first with two classes of Gentiles: those who already knew something of Jewish thought and culture, who knew and accepted something of the Jewish religious truth, and those who did not. Cornelius had been of the first class. To him Peter could say:

"You know what took place throughout Judea. Jesus of Nazareth began in Galilee after the baptism preached by John. You know how God anointed him with the Holy Spirit and with power, and he went about doing good and healing all who were in the power of the devil because God was with him. We are witnesses of all that he did in the country of the Jews and in Jerusalem. Yet they killed him, hanging him on a cross. But God raised him on the third day and caused him to be plainly seen, not by all the people but by witnesses designated beforehand by God, that is, by us, who ate and drank with him after he had risen from the dead. Jesus also charged us to preach to the people and to bear witness that he it is who has been appointed by God to be judge of the living and the dead. To him all the prophets bear witness that through his name all who believe in him may receive forgiveness of sins" (Acts 10, 37–43).

Peter's explanation presupposes that Cornelius has heard something of John the Baptist and of Jesus. And his reference to "all the prophets" seems to imply that Cornelius also knows something of Jewish tradition and expectations.

But even for such a Gentile, comparatively familiar with Jewish background, there has taken place a shift in emphasis in the account of Jesus. The central fact is still there, exactly as it was in the accounts to the Jews: Jesus, pointed out by John, was marked out by God as God's special and chosen representative, bearer of God's Spirit; he went about teaching and doing good. But the Jews, rejecting him, had him put to death. God raised him up, and ordains him now as judge of the living and the dead and gives forgiveness of sins through him.

It is in the last point that the shift in emphasis lies. Now the account no longer ends simply: God has fulfilled the promises to Israel in Jesus — promises of resurrection from the dead, outpouring of the Spirit, and freedom from sin. Now they say: God actually gives these things, these same promised good things, through Christ to "everyone who believes in him." Christianity stands clearly revealed for the world religion that it is. Peter can rightly say, "Now I really understand that God shows no partiality, but in every nation the man that fears him and does what is right is acceptable to him" (Acts 10, 34–35).

The first record of the preaching to the other sort of Gentile, those who were still untouched by Jewish thought and the Old Testament revelation, is St. Paul's sermon at Lystra in Asia Minor, recorded in the fourteenth chapter of Acts. To them he says: "We bring to you the Good News that you should turn from these vain gods to the living God who made heaven and earth and the sea and all things that are in them" (Acts 14, 15).

A later sermon at Athens is to the same class of hearer:

"What . . . you worship unknowingly, I make known to you. God, who made the world and all that is in it, since he is Lord of heaven and earth, does not dwell in temples built by hands. . . . We ought not to imagine that the Divinity is like to gold or silver or stone, to an image graven by human art and thought. The time of this ignorance, God, it is true, viewed with indulgence, but now he calls on all men everywhere to have a change of mind and heart, inasmuch as he has fixed a day on which he will judge the world with justice through a Man whom he has appointed. He has given proof of this to all by raising him from the dead" (Acts 17, 23, 29–31).

These show that for the Gentiles who were still idolaters the first message had to be the same basic attempt at conversion to the one true God which any Jewish preacher would have had to undertake. But there was a difference between the message that Paul and a Jewish proselytizer had to communicate. This lay in Paul's additional message that this one true God, who had "in many fragmentary and various utterances spoken of old through the prophets," has now, in "the final epoch . . . spoken to us through his Son, whom he has appointed heir of the universe" (Heb 1, 1–2). Salvation is available through faith in him, to all who believe. The good news "is the power of God to bring about salvation for everyone that has faith, for Jew first and then Greek. For in it God's way of sanctifying by an ever increasing faith is revealed. As it is written, 'The holy man lives by faith'" (Rom 1, 16–17).

An example of how the message could be summed up in this way, even for Gentiles of completely pagan background, occurs in the sixteenth chapter of Acts. Paul is in prison in Philippi, in Greek territory. An earthquake terrifies the jailer who has charge of Paul, and the man cries out: "What must I do to be saved?" The answer: "Believe in the Lord Jesus and you and your household shall be saved" (Acts 16, 31). That this was only a summary is clear from the fact that Paul went on to "speak the word of the Lord to him" that night and to baptize him. But the point of the most dramatic moment of the account is clearly not a matter of belonging to this nation or that, nor even taking on Jewish law and ritual, but of making an act of faith in the Lord Jesus.

This becomes a motto for St. Paul, who takes up the special mission of preaching to the non-Jews. It is echoed and reechoed again and again in his epistles. There is a new plan of salvation revealed by God. It is open to all the world and to all men everywhere. And one enters upon it by an act of faith in Jesus.

This then becomes the new note of the message as preached to the Gentiles: in Jesus is a whole new way of salvation for men, and this way is available to all men. As a matter of fact this way of faith is the only way of salvation even for the Jews, for whom Jesus also fulfilled the promises made of old. In brief everyone, even the Jew who wishes simply to enter into the promises which are the proper inheritance of his race, can enter upon them only by the way of faith in Jesus.

True, this latter point regarding the Jews can be seen already in Peter's words on Pentecost day: "What shall we do?" "Have a change of heart and mind and be baptized every one of you in the name of Jesus Christ for the remission of your sins" (Acts 2, 37–38). But the preaching to the Gentiles and the defense of the Gentiles against ultraconservative Jewish Christians gradually made it fully clear that in this very point lay the essence of their good news: faith, not blood descent from Abraham, and not fidelity to the law of Moses, but faith in Jesus brought a man into the family of the saved, the new Israel.

This was so revolutionary an idea and so central in its importance that it soon had to occupy a large part of the theme of many of Paul's letters, especially Romans and Galatians. In these Paul had to justify this new line of approach which had become associated above all with his name. Still, he did so with full approval of the apostolic community, as is made clear in the record in Acts of the Council of Jerusalem and in his own report in Galatians. The arguments he uses reflect the Christian rethinking of the Old Testament and largely set the pattern for the Church's new under-standing of the Old Testament in all future ages. We shall look at some of them briefly in Chapter 11.

But what, for the Gentiles, could take the place of the Jews' promises? Nothing could really. And so part of the full training of a Christian, even a Gentile, was education in the Old Testament, and finally the explanation that through faith in Christ he too could become an heir of the promises. But an initial announcement to a Gentile audience could not presuppose familiarity with the Old Testament. For an introduction to the "good news" the apostles came to rely more and more on the notion of "salvation." Just as the "promises" for the Jews had come to stand in a general way for the sum of all possible good things, so had the idea "salvation" in the Hellenistic world in which St. Paul's Gentiles lived.

Saved? From what would a person want to be saved? Why, from all things in life he has found unpleasant: the hardship, the pain, the drudgery of daily existence; the sufferings from sickness, from age, from the cruelty and selfishness of other men; the worry about tomorrow, the fear of greater evils yet to come, fear of evil spirits, the fear of the greatest and surest evil of them all, one's own death. Liberation from anything a man might fear or suffer or regret — his own helplessness, and, above all — if he understood himself correctly — from his own sins, his own sickness of soul, selfishness, shortsightedness, cruelty, uncontrollable lusts. This is what "salvation" in general meant in that world. And to find it, men of that day created for themselves salvation gods, redeemers and strange mystery rites through which such salvation could be found and purchased. Even the Roman emperor gloried in the title of "savior."

Again, to the extent that particular groups knew of or believed in a life after death, a future existence of some unknown sort for themselves or at least for their souls, salvation included too, quite naturally, an assurance of well-being in that life to come.

All these notions or something very much like them must have been in the mind of any Gentile who heard it preached that Jesus Christ was the Savior of mankind, that he saved us from sin, that he was God's promised salvation to all who believe in him. Hence, when the apostles testified that these things were so, that Jesus had claimed to be such a salvation, that God had made him manifest as such, that God had already worked salvation in him by raising him from the dead — that he was in this resurrection merely the firstborn among many brethren, that we too could all share in the same salvation by sharing in his cross and resurrection, this was a wonderful message of good news, an answer to all the human heart most longed for.

Moreover, the apostolic community and new converts as well could testify from their own experience and show in their lives that as a matter of fact God did work salvation in and through them. They could testify that in their midst, by way of a sign, the sick were healed and the dead raised, that the Holy Spirit of God was poured forth upon the ordinary members of the community, enabling them to enter upon a new life with a new and real joy and peace, despite the most awful trials and persecutions. As a result, it became obvious to those who listened to them and saw them that here was a reality indeed, a true and palpable human triumphing over sickness and evil and sin and death.

It is not surprising, in light of all this, that so many Gentiles saw the Christian message as good news indeed and flocked to the Church in order to receive through faith in Christ their own proper share in it all.

CHAPTER 4

The Message

WE HAVE seen the message as it was preached to the Jews. We have seen it preached to the Gentiles. Can we now line up more exactly the elements contained in it and try to study them in themselves? This has its dangers: elements given in a concrete and living situation cannot be pulled out of it for separate examination without undergoing some damage. Yet analysis is necessary, in this case as in most. As we perform the analysis in this and the next few chapters, however, we must be constantly mindful that in spite of all our close application we are not really seeing the whole story or even the true story, until in Chapter 12 we start trying to put things together again.

Let us begin again from the texts which record the earliest preaching:

"Jesus of Nazareth was a man accredited to you by God through miracles and wonders and signs, which God did through him in your midst, as you yourselves know. When he was delivered up by the settled purpose and foreknowledge of God, you crucified and slew him by the hands of wicked men. But God has raised him up. . . . Of that fact we all are witnesses" (Acts 2, 22–24, 32).

"[Jesus] you indeed delivered up and disowned in the presence of Pilate, when he had decided to release him. You, however, disowned the Holy and Just One, and asked that a murderer be released to you; but you killed the leader of life, whom God has raised from the dead. Of this fact we are witnesses" (Acts 3, 13–15).

"The God of our fathers raised Jesus, whom you put to death, hanging him on a gibbet. . . . And we are witnesses of these events" (Acts 5, 30, 32).

"God anointed him [Jesus of Nazareth] with the Holy Spirit and with power, and he went about doing good and healing all who were in the power of the devil because God was with him. We are witnesses to all that he did in the country of the Jews and in Jerusalem. Yet they killed him, hanging him on a cross. But God raised him on the third day and caused him to be plainly seen, not by all the people, but by witnesses designated beforehand by God, that is, by us, who ate and drank with him after he had risen from the dead" (Acts 10, 38–41).

"Really the citizens of Jerusalem and their leaders fulfilled the words of the prophets which are read every Sabbath by condemning Jesus in their ignorance. Though they found no grounds for the death penalty, they asked Pilate to have him put to death. And when they had carried out all that had been written concerning him, he was taken down from the cross and laid in a tomb. But God raised him from the dead; and he was seen during many days by those who had come up with him from Galilee to Jerusalem. So they became witnesses of him to the people" (Acts 13, 27–31).

The common elements in all these accounts are clear. First of all, they announce a fact, something which had happened, and of which the apostles themselves were witnesses. They present it clearly as an historical actuality, something which really occurred, something which they had "seen with their eyes, and looked upon and touched with their hands. . . ." Jesus of Nazareth, this good man, this "just one," this prophet, a man marked out by God, had been rejected by his own people and unjustly put to death.

They had lived with Jesus during all his public life. They knew how holy and just he really was. They had seen the good works and the healings he had done. They had listened to his teachings, that were like those of the prophets of old, and more. They had known what a horrible crime was being committed the night that Jesus was arrested, and though they fled at first in fear, later some — perhaps all — came back to stand helplessly somewhere nearby during his sufferings and execution.

But God had raised him from the dead. Of that they were witnesses too. For he "was seen during many days by those who had come up with him from Galilee to Jerusalem." "We ate and drank with him after he had risen from the dead."

Second, they proclaim God's purpose in what has happened. Jesus was "delivered up by the settled purpose and foreknowledge of God" (Acts 2, 23). "In this way God fulfilled what he had announced through all the prophets: that his Christ should suffer" (Acts 3, 18). "God according to promise brought to Israel a Savior, Jesus. . . . The citizens of Jerusalem and their leaders fulfilled the words of the prophets which are read every Sabbath by condemning Jesus in their ignorance" (Acts 13, 23, 27).

This last is a surprising note. They are not telling a wonder story, where wicked men have attacked God's hero and frustrated God's designs, and where God steps in at the end to save his own. Jesus was truly God's hero and wicked men did attack him, and human ignorance and human malice did do all they could to frustrate God's designs, just as they always do — but that was not the point. The point was that this greatest of human injustices, this extreme perversion of right order — that the best of men should meet the worst of fates — had all been done "by the settled purpose and foreknowledge of God."

This thought we will find repeated often in the New Testament, from John's "God so loved the world that he gave his only begotten Son" (Jn 3, 16) to Paul's "He did not spare his own Son but gave him up for us all" (Rom 8, 32). God sent him to die, and God raised him from the dead. And this is presented as good news. This means the fulfillment of the promises for Israel; this means salvation for the nations. Why? They do not yet say why. They are only stating the facts.

How did they know that this had all happened by the purpose and design of God? They would know it, first, from Jesus' words while he was still with them. Each of the four gospels devotes a large section to his attempts to instruct them in what is going to happen to him and what it will mean. They would know it, second, from the insight into Scripture which they received from the risen Jesus: "Then he interpreted to them whatever is said about himself anywhere in the Scriptures" (Lk 24, 27). "He opened their minds to understand the Scriptures" (Lk 24, 45). They would know it, third, from the fact that God had raised Jesus from the dead, thus justifying all his claims. They would know it, fourth, from general Jewish teaching about God, the same in this respect as sound natural theology leads to — that, hard as it is for us to understand how this can be, it is nevertheless true that everything, even the free acts of men, are dependent on the knowledge and will of God, and that God knowingly permits even men's evil actions in order to draw from them a greater good. And, finally, they would know it from the insight they received in the Holy Spirit into how what had happened to Jesus was really a message for all men.

The third element common to all these sermons is the direct application of the facts recounted to the hearers' own lives. Our outline sermons do not give any detailed account of how what has happened to Jesus is a message to the world. The apostles will do that abundantly in their teaching later and leave it to us in the epistles and the four gospels. But here they quickly draw three conclusions, which, as we shall see later, are really three aspects of one conclusion: repent, believe, be baptized.

" 'Brothers, what shall we do?' 'Have a change of heart and mind, and be baptized everyone of you in the name of Jesus Christ' " (Acts 2, 37–38).

"Have a change of heart, therefore; be converted" (Acts 3, 19).

"God exalted him . . . to grant a change of heart and mind . . ." (Acts 5, 31).

"Through his name all who believe in him may receive forgiveness of sin" (Acts 10, 43).

"To the Gentiles too God has given a change of heart and mind leading to life" (Acts 11, 18).

"Be it known to you, therefore, brothers, that it is by him that forgiveness of sins is proclaimed to you, and through this one everybody who believes is acquitted of all the sins of which you

could not be aquitted by the Law of Moses. Beware, therefore, that what is said in the prophets may not prove true of you,
> 'See you despisers, then wonder and perish,
> because I do a deed in your days.
> A deed which you will not believe,
> if anyone relates it to you' " (Acts 13, 38–41).

" 'What must I do to be saved?' 'Believe in the Lord Jesus . . . and you and your household shall be saved.' Paul and Silas spoke the word of the Lord to him and to all that were in his household. . . . Then and there he and his family were baptized" (Acts 16, 31–34).

What do they mean by these terms? Repent from what? Believe in what exactly, and why? What is the meaning of baptism? We shall try to answer these questions at greater length in the next chapter, but for the moment perhaps we can express it as follows: the apostles are calling their hearers to accept as true this strange and jarring message ("To the Jews indeed a stumbling block and to the Gentiles foolishness") that the story they have just heard is the story of God's salvation. This crucified man is the long-awaited Messiah. This is the Savior of the World, and this is the way God saves the world from the evils the world has gotten itself into. Accepting this fact and all that it implies, seeing God's hand in Christ's subjection to suffering and death and in his resurrection, and seeing God's purpose in it for all of us (faith), they "have a change of mind and heart," turn from sin to God (repentance), and declare openly by a public ceremonial act which will mark them out as his followers (baptism) their allegiance to a crucified and risen Lord.

In giving the above New Testament quotations for this third point, which we have just been examining, we could not always cut the words off from other words which applied strictly to the fourth element, the one we shall look at now. For instance:

"Through his name all who believe in him may receive forgiveness of sins" (Acts 10, 43). Forgiveness of sins, the apostles promise, will follow upon repentance, faith, baptism. "To the Gentiles too God has given a change of heart and mind leading to life" (Acts 11, 18). "Change of heart and mind" is the repentance; "leading to life" refers to the promised reward.

Similarly in the quotation from St. Paul: "everybody who believes is acquitted of all the sins of which you could not be acquitted by the Law of Moses" (Acts 13, 39).

Each of the other sermon summaries has the same fourth element, the good which they will receive by repentance, faith, baptism: "be baptized in the name of Jesus Christ for the remission of your sins; then you will receive the gift of the Holy Spirit" (Acts 2, 38).

"To grant a change of mind and heart and forgiveness of sins to Israel" (Acts 5, 31).

The fourth element, the gift which will be granted to those who repent, believe, accept baptism, is phrased variously as forgiveness of sins, life, receiving the Holy Spirit, and — in most general terms — the promises. "The promise is meant for you and for your children and for all who are afar off, for all whom the Lord our God may call to himself" (Acts 2, 39). It is also "being saved," as in the sentence after Peter's first speech: "With many other words he bore witness and exhorted them saying, 'Save yourselves from this perverse generation'" (Acts 2, 40).

We said above that they do not stop to tell exactly why this message about Christ is good news. That is not exactly true. They do not stop to discuss the point because the rest of what they are going to say will bring out that it is good news, and why (although only in very brief outline). They do not stop to theologize on the point. But they do communicate to their hearers the fact that Christ's death and resurrection are the foundation of everything that comes afterward. It is in Christ as having died and risen that one must believe. And it is because one gains some insight into the fact that the Christ, God's chosen, God's only Son, was crucified and rose that one repents and changes in mind and heart. It is allegiance to a living Messiah, who died as the crucified one, which a man proclaims in accepting baptism in his name.

And from repentance, faith, and baptism — grounded as these are in Christ's act — they announce there will come to the individual those good things he most wants and has need of: forgiveness of sins, the gift of the Spirit, the path to life, salvation from a perverse generation, the promises.

Would they have phrased the promised good things differently if they had been talking to a different group in a different age? Possibly. But perhaps not. "The gift of the Spirit" might not sound like a very stirring promise, but it would have sounded differently to those who saw the gift of the Spirit in action before their eyes. Simon Magus, not a very lofty-minded sort of character, was so impressed by it that he offered the apostles money and lent his name permanently to the repulsive sin of simony, in hope that he too might have the power of passing on that gift (Acts 8, 14–24).

"The forgiveness of sin" has an appeal perhaps only where a certain amount of spiritual sensitivity already exists in the audience. Most of the Jews would have that and appreciate it. As to the Gentiles, cases would vary. Perhaps it is deliberate that another point is added even in the address to Cornelius: "Jesus also charged us to preach to the people and to bear witness that it is he who has been appointed by God to be judge of the living and the dead" (Acts 10, 42). In the address at Athens the same note is struck: Paul has spoken of men seeking for God and "perhaps finding him as they grope after him," of their "gods of gold and silver and stone," but he adds: "The time of this ignorance, God, it is true, viewed with indulgence, but now he calls on all men everywhere to have a change of mind and heart, inasmuch as he has fixed a day on which he will judge the world with justice through a Man whom he has appointed. He has given proof of this to all by raising him from the dead" (Acts 17, 22–31).

Paul's address at Lystra seems headed down the same line when it is interrupted: "In the generations that are passed he let all the nations follow their own ways . . ." (Acts 14, 16).

"Life," "being saved" — understood in a general way as rescue from all that is evil — probably has a universal appeal. At any rate, what words might have been used in other situations we can only guess. Actually in the very first sermons occur only these few. But again we must remind ourselves that these sermons in

Acts are nothing but slender outlines. The full development of their ideas we find only in the epistles and the other New Testament writings.

We shall develop the third element — repentance, faith, and baptism — in Chapter 5, as we mentioned. The fourth element — the new life, the inheritance, salvation, the gift of the Spirit and forgiveness of sin which result — we shall take up in Chapters 6 to 11. These two elements, the third and the fourth together, are really an explanation of what is meant by the second element as it was preached: what happened, happened by God's design — that is, it was for your good. And of course all these elements together, as we have already seen, draw their meaning from the first, the thing that had really occurred and to which the apostles were ready to bear witness unto death — the unjust death and the glorious resurrection of Jesus the Christ.

THE WORD IN THE TEACHING

CHAPTER 5

Repentance, Faith, Baptism

REPENTANCE, faith, and baptism made up what we have called the third element in the good news as it was first preached. Together they gave the immediate answer to the question, What must I do? which people asked spontaneously when they heard what had happened to Jesus, and heard of God's plan in that happening. They are the first thing demanded of those who hear the message: repentance and belief, the internal response; baptism, its external symbolic expression.

As we begin studying them, a double caution is perhaps in order. The first is to remember that we are analyzing this triple response as it was called for in the preaching. That means we are approaching it, so to say, from the human side, examining its psychological and symbolic elements, looking for what the first hearers understood was expected of themselves. There is another whole side to repentance, faith, and baptism, a sense in which they are pure gifts of God. The New Testament recognizes and teaches this sense. But in the context of the preaching, as outlined in Acts, these three are the object of exhortation; that is, they tell what is expected from the listener, not from God.

Second, it is good before beginning this analysis to remind ourselves once more of the danger of taking any one part of what we are studying as if it were the whole. No one part alone is the "real meaning" of the message. Or rather, every part is the real meaning — but only when seen in perspective as one part or aspect of the whole. Ultimately we will try to reunite the parts again into a single whole the way that the Church herself did in that apostolic age.

To begin with, the person who has heard the preaching of the message is called on to repent. Repent: be sorry for the past, resolve to be different in the future. The Greek word used in the New Testament text indicates a change of mind, heart, attitude; the Hebrew biblical equivalent stands for a turning around or back, a conversion. But change and conversion imply, just as the English word "repentance," a turning away from the past, regretting it if it was bad, and replacing it with what is new and good.

"Repent and be baptized every one of you in the name of Jesus Christ." "Repent therefore and turn yourselves around." "Sent to preach repentance to the Jews and to the Gentiles."

What is this repentance? What did one have to give up, turn from, change? First of all, of course, repentance bears upon obvious and known sin where that is present and recognized. Renouncing deliberate offense against God would naturally be a first step toward entering a new order which was all from God.

But repentance goes deeper than this. Many of those who first eagerly heard the word were devout Jews who were doing their best to observe God's law. For their sins of weakness they were already sorry; faithful practice of their own religion and devout reading of Scripture taught them this much. For them a stirring call to repentance had to penetrate to deeper recesses of the human heart, to levels where all men at the center of their being realize that all is not right between them and God, where they feel unsure about the forgiveness of things objectively wrong which they know they have done in the past, feel the uncleanness of daily temptation and their own weak hesitation in the face of it, feel unable to live up to the holiness of the all-pure God who they know both sees and judges their every most secret thought.

But even this does not explain fully the repentance called for by the New Testament, because this keen sense of sin, when genuine, is characteristic of a highly developed religious sensitivity and is not likely to be widely found. It could hardly be alone the successful basis for a general theme of preaching.

As directed to the Jews, the apostolic call for repentance was sometimes based on the collective guilt of the nation in rejecting and killing their appointed Messiah. But of course not all or even most of the hearers had had any real personal part in that sin, so that too does not suffice for a general explanation. Nor would it account for the preaching to the Gentiles.

We must then probably say that repentance bears on all the things we have mentioned to some extent. But its full meaning in this context probably is something still deeper, something which is a direct — and conscious — result of hearing the gospel message. It is a state of soul, an attitude toward one's own moral activity, which results directly from believing the gospel which has been preached. And so we must turn for a moment to the meaning of believing, of faith.

Hearing the gospel message, what are they being asked to believe? They are being asked to believe a fact and to believe in a person. The fact is this: Jesus died and rose from the dead, and this is our salvation. The person is Jesus the Christ; that is, the crucified and risen Lord of glory, and our Savior.

Let us consider first the fact. That Jesus had died, and that he was the just and innocent man the apostles claimed, who had done works which marked him out as God's prophet and chosen one, they either knew already or could find out from anyone who had known what actually happened. That Jesus had been seen alive again, they were being asked to take on the word of these witnesses who had seen him (Acts 10, 40–41). That this was God's chosen way of salvation, they had to take on God's word. This word was manifested, first, in Jesus himself, his life and teaching; second, in the fact that God had raised him from the dead; third, in the fact that the whole of Old Testament history and prophecy had, in the salvation pattern demonstrated throughout the long history of the people and in the exhortations and shadowings-forth of the future in the prophetic writings, pointed imperfectly to some such future perfect accomplishment; and, finally, in the evident fact that the apostolic community possessed the Spirit of God and performed the works of the Spirit.

If they accepted the fact as true, they were accepting something astounding, in itself incredible, scandalous — "a stumbling block, foolishness." That is, they were being called to accept the paradox that this is God's message of salvation, the divine answer to all their hopes, God's fulfillment of all his promises — a crucified, suffering, rejected, dying man. To accept him as Lord, to admit that God raised him up and glorified him *because* he had been God's perfect servant in his suffering ("obedient unto death, even the death of the cross; for which cause God has exalted him . . ." [Phil 2, 8–9]) was implicitly to overturn the human values normally accepted. It was to admit that God and truth and life come to man in this sinful world, not by the things men ordinarily pursue — esteem, possessions, security — but in the outrage, in the scandal of the cross.

The cross means resurrection, eternal life. But this is only for those who believe. For the rest, for the "carnal man" it is a horror. But the preaching is precisely a call on them to believe, to accept this as true because God has revealed it — that here on the cross God is working salvation: that the cross is even the sign and the seal of God's working, the normal badge of the just in this sinful world ("all who would live piously in Christ Jesus will suffer persecution" [2 Tm 3, 12]); and that only insofar as they can bring themselves to accept that message, will they enter into the new life, the life of the resurrection, the new age of the Anointed One, the kingdom of God.

But this is a scandal for natural reason; and the New Testament, as the whole later history of the Church, is full of that scandal. Thus they are being asked to change over to a whole new outlook on life, an outlook whose motto and reason for existence is acceptance of this cross as God's plan, and of cross-resurrection as God's design for salvation, with all that that will imply for their own lives too later on.

Second, let us consider the person in whom they are being asked to believe. The first sermons speak of him with great reverence and love: "a man accredited to you by God through miracles and wonders and signs which God did through him in your midst"

(Acts 2, 22); "God has made him both Lord and Christ, this very Jesus whom you have crucified" (Acts 2, 36); "God . . . has glorified his servant, Jesus, whom you indeed delivered up and disowned in the presence of Pilate, when he had decided to release him. You . . . disowned the Holy and Just One, and asked that a murderer be released to you. You killed the leader of life" (Acts 3, 13–15); "God anointed him with the Holy Spirit and with power, and he went about doing good and healing all who were in the power of the devil because God was with him" (Acts 10, 38); "John [the Baptist] said . . . 'One is coming after me, and I am not worthy to untie the shoes of his feet'" (Acts 13, 25); "Though they found no grounds for the death penalty, they asked Pilate to have him put to death" (Acts 13, 28).

These first sermons tell that Jesus fulfilled God's mission in what he did, especially in his death and resurrection. But to understand what faith in him meant, we have to go beyond these first sermons to other remarks scattered through the New Testament which show that they meditated from the first and preached from the first how he was himself an active agent in the great salvific events. These things did not just happen to him. He accepted the cross, he accepted death in conformity with God's design, because he was obedient to God's will in all things, and because he shared God's love for men.

Thus St. Paul writes not only "God is for us; who can be against us? He has not spared his only Son, but delivered him up for us all" (Rom 8, 32) but also, of Jesus, "he loved me and sacrificed himself for me" (Gal 2, 20). And, in Philippians, "he humbled himself and became obedient to death, yes, to death on a cross" (Phil 2, 8). And Peter: "'He committed no sin, and no deceit was found on his lips.' When he was insulted he did not return the insult; when he was mistreated, he did not threaten, but entrusted himself to him who judges justly" (1 Pt 2, 21–22). And John: "We know what love is from the fact that Jesus Christ laid down his life for us" (1 Jn 3, 16).

There is an emphasis on the way and the spirit, the dispositions in which Jesus had submitted himself to his fate. He had carried out God's plan for saving sinful men, submissive to the divine design, cooperating with it eagerly out of love for the Father and for men. That this emphasis was there from the beginning we can see even from the very earliest epistle we have, 1 Thessalonians. There Paul is not describing explicitly the way Christ met death, but his repeated exhortations to his readers in the first three chapters to bear persecution, suffering, afflictions, labors patiently, joyously, as "imitators of ourselves and of the Lord," clearly presuppose that he has explained to them in his preaching (which had lasted three weeks — Acts 17) Christ's patient endurance. In Chapter 4 of the same epistle he writes: "You have learned from God how to love one another."

And finally proof that Christ's dispositions in his suffering were recounted and meditated on from the very first days lies in the passion narratives in our gospels. For the passion narratives are older than the rest of the gospels. It is now recognized, moreover, that the passion was recounted in considerable detail in the very earliest liturgical services. That recounting soon took a fixed form, a form we see preserved in all four gospels today. The gospels differ less in the sequence and details of the passion than they do in any other section. Detailed study of the gospels belongs in a later chapter of this book, but to establish this one point it is important to look at them briefly now. They confirm what we have said and tried to show from the epistles, that from the first, considerable emphasis was placed on Jesus' subjective dispositions in accepting suffering and death as willed by his Father.

The Last Supper scene gives Jesus' words indicating that he knows what is about to happen to him and that he accepts it willingly and "for you." The garden scene centers on Jesus' prayer showing complete submission to the divine will. Before his judges he affirms his mission, he will not take back his claims. But when he is accused falsely, condemned, denied by his own, when he is imprisoned, subjected to mockery and blows, he bears it all in silence. He dies amid taunts for his claim to be God's chosen one and for his faithfulness and calm confidence in God in the midst of this. He prays for those who are doing this to him, comforts his friends, expresses his suffering in the word "I thirst" and in the psalm "My God, my God, why hast thou forsaken me." He gives up his soul into his Father's hands.

The first hearers are being asked to believe in this person as God's Messiah, as exalted to God's right hand, as Lord. Faith in him will mean putting all their hopes in him, as the apostles did during his lifetime. But now there is no vagueness about the direction in which these hopes lead. Believing in him will mean allegiance to him: he had said, "Follow me."

The first sermons probably could not have spelled all that out for them fully. But they must have made them feel it at least vaguely. There is a terrible reproach in the simple words "the Just One, whom you crucified." As they realize all that he endured in submission to God's will, and as they realize something of the love for them which moved him to do so, they cannot help being, like the crowd on Pentecost day, "touched to the heart."

God's standards and God's way of salvation had been pointed toward and hinted at in word or in act by all the true prophets. But never had they been set so clearly before men's eyes as in the cross and resurrection of Jesus. Men had lived good lives before and offered example to other men and pleased God by their obedience and charity in a way that helped offset the wickedness of many others. But never had there been an act of such flawless obedience and charity as this self-giving of Christ. And it had all been for them, that through repentance, faith, and baptism they might enter on true life and find salvation.

Their belief that this was true and the moving power of their faith in him would then naturally give them a new standard of values, a new picture of God and reality and the meaning of human life. In that light, their whole past lives would seem unworthy, would be seen for what they really had been: a running away from, a hiding from God's pattern, a clinging to false values which were felt as false for they never gave real satisfaction, and, no matter how noble, never seemed to come to actual grips with the problems of the world as it is. Consequently they would feel regret for the past and a keen sense of the need for making the future different.

What about their belief in the person of Christ as divine? Recent studies have shown that such expressions as "exalted to God's right hand," "sending forth the Holy Spirit upon us," and "Lord" did, in the mouths of the first-generation Christian Jews, objectively imply Christ's true divinity. To the extent to which the hearers of the first sermons actually perceived this truth, it would intensify everything we have described so far: the horror of their having rejected him, the condescension and the love which he showed, the faith and confidence which they could have in him. However they perceived it when they first heard the message, at least they knew it insofar as he "was designated the mighty Son of God by his resurrection from the dead" (Rom 1, 4).

Yet repentance and faith, the interior change alone, are not enough. Before the Sanhedrin in Acts 5 only repentance is mentioned: the sermon at Pisidian Antioch in Acts 13 speaks only of faith. But the Pentecost sermon in Acts 2 says, "Repent and be baptized," and the account to Cornelius (Acts 10, 43, 48) and that to the jailer at Philippi (Acts 16, 31, 33) link that belief immediately with baptism.

What was this baptism? The documents speak of it as a baptism in (or into) the name of the Lord Jesus. It was a washing of some sort; the very name baptism ("dipping") means at least that. And the physical action with water was accompanied by a profession of faith, given in a certain formula of words. One such formula seems to have been, "Jesus is Lord." This would be, in a few short words, a public acceptance of the whole of the Christian message and teaching. It would mean: the Crucified One is the Exalted One, and in him we have our salvation.

But why an external act at all? After all, the apostles, like Jesus himself, often criticized Jewish religious practice of their day for being too ready to let external rites and observances take the place of true religion of the heart. Yet their very first demand of those who would follow them is that they express their internal sentiments of faith and repentance in the external act of being baptized. And Christ willed it so. Why?

First of all, this is an example of something that comes up again and again in the New Testament as in the later history of the Church. It is the sacramental principle: God's action in man and man's response to God are essentially matters of the inmost heart; and yet God approaches the heart through external, material words and actions and objects, and the heart expresses its answer in a similar way. We shall look more fully into this external-internal relation in Chapter 10.

But second, the reason why faith and repentance had to be completed with the external symbol of baptism is that this new salvation was from the first not an individual but a community affair. Jesus had come from God as God's Messiah to save God's people. One who accepted God's message of salvation in Christ declared his faith and repentance openly, that he might be counted openly and before the world as a member of God's true people, the remnant of Israel which the prophets had foretold. We shall see more of this in Chapter 11.

Thus, in summary, baptism was looked on probably as an external act of washing, symbolizing repentance and the remission of sins. Second, it was a formal and public confession of faith in the name of Jesus — Jesus is Savior, Jesus is Lord, hence a public acceptance of the whole Christian revelation and Christian viewpoint on life. And third, baptism marked those who received it as members of the saved community, God's people, the true Israel, the Church which was being formed.

What reasons, apart from the command and example of Christ, might have led them to choose this particular sign? John the Baptist had already used it as a sign of repentance and conversion. The Qumran sectaries used it for initiation in much the same way. The rest of the Jews, too, knew it as an initiation rite accompanying circumcision for a convert from paganism. It was, then, at least a symbol of purification and renewal easily understood as such by all. And it was a known mark of initiation as well.

Christian baptism was more than all this. And yet Christian baptism could hardly have been cut off completely in the thought and feeling of those who practiced it from what they had done previously themselves and seen done by other pious Jews. There would be a good deal of carry-over.

We learn much about the fuller meaning of this rite for Christians from the New Testament epistles. Baptism, we have already seen, was the externalizing of the repentance and belief in the convert's heart. Christ's death and resurrection were the salvation of all who accepted them and the revelation of God contained in them. He who really believed wanted to enter into this salvation and the promises connected with it. So he publicly dedicated himself to them, in order, with all other believers, to accept a certain form for his life, God's way of salvation made known in Christ, the form of the salvation worked in Christ, the form of death and resurrection; and he accepted this, not just as one individual, but as a member of the people God was calling to himself in Christ.

The New Testament authors express these thoughts in terms learned from the Old Testament. That is, in the Old Testament, God's great act of salvation had been to call and lead the people of Israel out of slavery in Egypt, through the Red Sea, and to the holy mountain in the desert. There he made a personal pact with the people: he would be their God, they his people; and if they kept his Law, the statutes and ordinances connected with his treaty, God would bring them into the land he had promised to their fathers, a land flowing with milk and honey. If they remained faithful to that law: the ten commandments, the ceremonial statutes, other more detailed moral directives — they would go on enjoying prosperity, victory, peace, the possession of the land as the fulfillment of promises, and all good things.

This agreement was solemnly sealed by sacrifices offered and blood poured out and by the annual celebration of the Passover. Moreover each Jew, then and for all future generations, was to mark his acceptance of this covenant and all its obligations and signify his membership in God's people by undergoing circumcision.

The Christians applied this to God's final, Messianic salvation, which they were receiving from Christ. They had learned that God's greatest act of salvation was the death and resurrection of Christ. They understood that God was calling them, by faith in the cross and resurrection, out from slavery to sin to come to himself. He was forming for himself his own special people out of all those who would believe and accept his anointed one. Christ's death and resurrection announced a new covenant between God and man — a covenant which would save those who believed, a covenant of which the only laws would be "the law of faith" (Rom 3, 27), "the law of the Spirit of life in Christ Jesus" (Rom 8, 2). (Cf. next section on the Spirit, and the following chapters.)

This agreement between God and man was not only proclaimed, it was also solemnly inaugurated and sealed in Christ's self-offering on the cross, and by his blood poured out. And it was confirmed by God's raising him from the dead. These were the great events of Good Friday and Easter, the Christian Passover. Every individual who would declare his allegiance to this covenant and mark himself permanently as a member of God's people in Christ, professed his faith publicly by accepting baptism, which initiated him into the new people.

Thus we read: "all of us who have been baptized into union with Christ Jesus have been baptized into union with his death. Yes, we were buried in death with him by means of baptism, in order that, just as Christ was raised from the dead by the glorious power of the Father, so we also may conduct ourselves by a new principle of life. Now since we have grown to be one with him through a death like his, we shall also be one with him by a resurrection like his" (Rom 6, 3-5). "In union with him you have received the circumcision of Christ, not a circumcision administered by hand, but that which consists in cutting away our sinful nature. Buried with him by baptism, you also rose with him by your faith in the power of God who raised him from the dead" (Col 2, 11-12).

"You are . . . all children of God through faith in Jesus Christ, since all of you who have come to Christ by baptism have clothed yourselves with Christ. . . . And if you are Christ's, then you are the offspring of Abraham, heirs according to the promise" (Gal 3, 27–29).

The first epistle of Peter, recognized as treating throughout of Paschal and baptismal themes, says: "This honor therefore is for you who believe. . . . You are a chosen race, a royal priesthood, a holy nation, a people that is God's possession . . . " (1 Pt 2, 7–9).

This fact, that in baptism they accepted Christ and the new way of life in him, becomes in many of the New Testament letters a favored starting place and basis for exhortations to living the crucified and risen life of a Christian. It is the basis of a whole new moral order. "That I may gain Christ, and be found united to him, not with a holiness of my own derived from the Law, but with that which is obtained by faith in Christ, the holiness which God imparts on condition of faith. I would know Christ and what his resurrection can do. I would also share in his sufferings, in the hope that if I resemble him in death, I may somehow attain to the resurrection from the dead" (Phil 3, 9–10).

This concern of the apostles is reflected in such statements as: "If you have risen with Christ, seek the things that are above . . . " (Col 3, 1); "You have died. . . . Therefore put to death the passions which belong to earth . . ." (Col 3, 5); etc. We shall see more of these later.

*   *   *

At the very beginning of the book of Acts, Jesus, about to depart from his disciples for the last time, says, "You shall be baptized with the Holy Spirit not many days hence" (Acts 1, 5). This promise came true on the first Pentecost. From that point on, the book of Acts, which is a story of the early years and first growth of the Church, becomes what has been called the "gospel of the Spirit." This Spirit, which we saw descend on the apostles that first day of the public life of the Church, is promised to all who will believe and be baptized. The Spirit comes as one of the chief fulfillments of the ancient divine promises.

We saw the prophecy of Joel which Peter quotes in his first

sermon: "I will pour forth my spirit on all mankind, and your sons and daughters shall prophesy. . . . " The prophet Ezekiel had written, foretelling the Messianic age: "A new heart will I give you, and a new spirit will I put within you. I will take out of your flesh the heart of stone, and give you a heart of flesh. And I will put my Spirit within you, and cause you to walk in my statutes, and you shall observe my ordinances. You shall dwell in the land which I gave to your fathers, and you shall be my people, and I will be your God" (Ez 36, 26–28). And in the following chapter, Ezekiel is granted the vision of the field of dry bones. At the word of the Lord, "Come from the four winds, O Spirit, and breathe upon these slain that they may live," the bones, covered over with flesh, return to life.

> "Then he said to me: 'Son of man, these bones are the whole house of Israel. Behold they say, Our bones are dried up, and our hope is lost and we are cut off. Therefore prophesy and say to them, Thus says the Lord God: Behold I will open your graves and raise you up from your graves, O my people. And I will bring you home into the land of Israel. And you shall know that I am the Lord, when I open your graves and raise you from your graves, O my people. And I will put my Spirit within you and you shall live. And I will place you in your own land. Then you shall know that I the Lord have spoken and performed it, says the Lord."

This is the same Spirit foretold in Isaiah: "The Spirit of the Lord shall rest upon him, the spirit of wisdom and understanding, the spirit of counsel and might, the spirit of knowledge and of fear of the Lord" (Is 11, 2). Isaiah is speaking of the Messiah to come. Of him he also writes: "The Spirit of the Lord God is upon me, because the Lord has anointed me to bring good tidings to the afflicted; he has sent me to bind up the brokenhearted, to proclaim liberty to the captives and the opening of the prison to those who are bound . . . " (Is 61, 1–2).

The "gift of the Spirit" becomes in the New Testament one way of referring to the whole new life in Christ. The Spirit is in individuals, he is in the community. He gives understanding of Scripture and the ability and courage to bear testimony to the truth and to preach. The Spirit is the source of the freedom from sin which they experience — both the remission of past sins and the new strength to avoid sin in the present and future.

The Spirit is the Author of the strange gifts of the charisms — "The manifestation of the Spirit is given to each individual for the common good. For example, to one is imparted the ability to speak with wisdom, to another with knowledge under the guidance of the same Spirit, to another by the same Spirit is imparted wonder-working confidence, to another gifts of healing by the one Spirit, to another the performance of miracles, to another inspired preaching, to another the discernment of spirits, to another the ability to speak in various languages, to another the ability to interpret them. But it is one and the same Spirit who is active in all these gifts, which he distributes just as he wishes" (1 Cor 12, 7–11). He is also the Author of the hierarchical structure of the community:

> There is one body and one Spirit, just as you, from the moment you were called, had the one hope your calling imparted. There is one Lord, one faith, one baptism, one God and Father of all. . . . But to each of us grace has been given to the extent to which Christ imparts it. . . . He established some men as apostles, and some as inspired spokesmen, others again as evangelists, and others as pastors and teachers, thus organizing the saints for the work of the ministry . . . (Eph 4, 4–12).

Yet a very real unity underlies all these different activities of the Spirit. He was foretold as resting in the first place upon the Messiah. And so in the sermon in Acts 10, Peter speaks of "how God anointed Jesus of Nazareth with the Holy Spirit and with power." The Holy Spirit was first and above all "the Spirit of Christ," the "Spirit of Jesus." The unity underlying the activities of the Spirit in the individual Christian and in the whole Church is this: those who make the act of accepting Christ and God's word in him, interiorly by faith, exteriorly by baptism, receive as a pure gift of God a share in this same Spirit of Christ, which will enable them to do in some measure what Christ did, be in some measure what Christ was, and gradually, more and more perfectly to bear Christ's image.

You, however, are not sensual but spiritual, since the Spirit of God really dwells in you, whereas no one who is deprived of the Spirit of Christ belongs to Christ. But if Christ is in you, the body, it is true, is destined to death because of sin, but the spirit has life because of its holiness (Rom 8, 9–11).

Whoever are led by the Spirit of God, they are the sons of God. . . . You have received a spirit of adoption as sons, in virtue of which we cry, "Abba! Father!" . . . We are children of God. But if we are children, we are heirs also: heirs indeed of God and joint heirs with Christ, since we suffer with him that we may also be glorified with him. . . . Those whom he [God] has foreknown he has also predestined to be conformed to the image of his Son, so that this Son should be the first-born among many brethren (Rom 8, 14–17, 29–30).

You are, . . . all children of God through faith in Jesus Christ, since all of you who have come to Christ by baptism have clothed yourselves with Christ . . . You are all one in Christ Jesus (Gal 3, 27–29).

. . . By a single Spirit all of us, whether Jews or Greeks, slaves or free men, were introduced into the one body through baptism (1 Cor 12, 13).

Strip off the old self with its deeds and put on the new, which is being progressively remolded after the image of its Creator and brought to deep knowledge. Here there is no Gentile, no Jew, no circumcised, no uncircumcised, no barbarian, no Scythian, no slave, no free man, but Christ is everything in each of us (Col 3, 10–11).

. . . God . . . has established us firmly along with you in communion with Christ, and has anointed us, and stamped us with his seal, and given us the Spirit as the first installment of what is to come (2 Cor 1, 21–22).

We shall explore more fully in the following chapters this image of Christ produced in the believer and in the Church by the Spirit. We shall look at it especially as it manifests itself in the bearing of the cross as Christ bore his: "if indeed we suffer with him that we may also be glorified with him" (Rom 8, 17); and in loving as he loved: "The love of God is poured forth in our hearts by the Spirit of God who is given to us" (Rom 5, 5). "The love of Christ drives me on" (2 Cor 5, 14).

*   *   *

To summarize then what we have seen: the basic message can be stated in the few words of the kerygma as we saw it in the earlier preaching and summarized it in the first chapters. Jesus, God's chosen and anointed one, came from God, taught the truth, did good; for this he was rejected by his people, handed over to the Romans and crucified. This was done according to God's foreknowledge and plan for the salvation of men. Jesus accepted it as such, out of obedience to God, out of love for men. God raised him from the dead, glorified him at his own right hand. This risen Jesus appeared to chosen witnesses and sent them forth to bear testimony to himself. And from heaven he sends upon those witnesses and upon those who believe them his own Spirit, God's Spirit, who brings them into a new way of life — a life in which they stand in right relation to God, sins forgiven, and in which they are enabled to live in submission to God and perfect love of men after the example of Christ. The Spirit given to the believers with baptism enables them to make Christ's way the model of their own, enables them to rise above sin and suffering and death to holiness, resurrection, and eternal life: first, from day to day, all their lives long, in ever increasing measure; and, second, in a perfect way, when Christ comes again at the last day for the resurrection of their bodies, the judgment of the living and the dead, and the final consummation of all things.

CHAPTER 6

Suffering

FROM the earliest apostolic letters to the latest, a strange linking of certain ordinarily unlinkable words takes place, words like "rejoicing in tribulation," "rejoicing in sorrow," "exulting in suffering," etc.

In his earliest letter, the first to the Thessalonians, St. Paul writes "You also followed our example and the Lord's, when, in great affliction, you welcomed the message and experienced the joy the Holy Spirit imparts. Thus you became a model to all believers in Macedonia and Achaia" (1, 6–7). In Romans, the phrase is "we exult in tribulations also, aware that tribulation produces endurance, endurance proven virtue, and proven virtue hope . . . " (5, 3–4). And in 2 Corinthians we read, "I overflow with joy over all our troubles" (7, 4). Again, in Colossians Paul writes: "I rejoice now in the sufferings I bear for your sake" (1, 29).

Peter, too, echoes these ideas: "Rejoice to the extent that you share in the sufferings of Christ" (1 Pt 4, 13). Actually, this theme is summed up in the last discourse, in St. John's gospel, where Jesus, after reviewing all that the hatred of the world will bring upon the apostles in the form of persecutions and martyrdoms, tells them he has said all this for their peace and for their joy. It is a sharing with Christ what the world has done and does to him. And so in Acts, after the first trial of the apostles before the authorities of the Jewish people, they come out, having been scourged and warned for the future, "rejoicing that they had been counted worthy to suffer disgrace for the name of Jesus" (5, 41).

We recognize this doctrine of course. We learn it today when as children we first hear the story of the cross. We know it from the beatitudes of the Sermon on the Mount: Happy are you when you suffer persecution for justice' sake. We know it from the story of the martyrs, so often eagerly going to persecution and death, and insisting that in the midst of their pains they experience the most intense consolation.

We know that this plays a regular role in the ascetical and mystical teaching of the Church. We recognize it as the hunger for suffering of St. Teresa of Avila and John of the Cross, as the Third Mode of Humility in the *Spiritual Exercises* of St. Ignatius.

What we do not perhaps always recognize is how immediately this attitude follows from the preaching of the cross and resurrection of Christ, and indeed not arbitrarily, or as a possibility of high spirituality, but necessarily for anyone who has really heard that word of the foolishness and the glory of the cross. Nor do we always advert to how prominent a place this idea held in the thinking of the first Christian community, and how much it is stressed in the apostolic letters and all the rest of the New Testament. And we do not always appreciate how distinctive this is of Christianity, and how, once put into practice, it makes all the difference for the reality of daily living.

Add to this all the references to "consolation in sufferings," and "as you share in sufferings, so shall you in the consolations," and "the sufferings of this life are not worthy to be compared to the glory that is to come," and one sees how central this becomes, how often it appears at every level of writing and in every period.

For suffering, evil, death, are in no way a peculiarly Christian problem. Every religion, every important philosophy, has to wrestle with them, not only to "justify the ways of God to men" but to make man's life livable, psychologically possible, here on earth.

The problems of sin, suffering, and death force themselves upon every thinking consciousness. One may not know or find an answer to them except finally to shrug one's shoulders and seek to escape them somehow. Escape them one cannot. To shrug one's shoulders is possible. It does not help very much. But one way or another, everyone must react. No one can pretend for very long that these problems do not exist.

So it is not Christianity which creates the problems. The problems are there, in the real world. And every thinker, and therefore every theology and philosophy to some extent or other, concern themselves with them.

One particularly pressing and sharp statement of the problem is felt by the religions and ethical systems of the highest morality. It is the problem of the suffering of the just man — "Why should a good man be afflicted in life, and what is the point of goodness if it is not productive of happiness and long life?" Put another way, it is the simple problem of the difficulty of long perseverance in the good life.

To explain this last point: every man has his problems. But the man who undertakes to live a good life, according to any of the higher moral systems, exposes himself to certain special problems. His goal may be greater happiness, but the road to that goal runs through a considerable degree of self-restraint, self-control, privation. His temptation, lasting as long as he tries to persevere in good, will be: "Why go to so much trouble? No one else does." And others who seek their own ease and pleasure and profit seem happier and more blessed than he. As the attempt to practice good stretches out over a long period of time, this temptation can become stronger and stronger. Add to it the persecutions of the wicked, the fact that the unscrupulous take willing advantage of the delicate conscience, and it becomes clear that there is a specially keen twist, pain, in the problem of suffering and evil for the person trying to be good in a higher way, say in that of the Jewish religion before Christ.

At any rate, the problem, as we said, is given; it is not peculiar to Christianity. But the answer is. The answer is distinctive of Christianity, simply first because the answer lies in a complete grasp of what we have called the central message and revelation of Christianity. It results immediately from a true and correct faith in the announcement that Jesus Christ died on the cross for our sins and rose again for our justification.

How so? Let us recall what a man accepts as true when he makes the act of faith in the message: Jesus is Lord, Jesus, dying on the cross for us, is our salvation. He accepts first of all the general background principle, known already to the Old Testament revelation, that suffering and death are in the world because of man's sin. Second, he faces the fact that in this concrete, real world where sin does reign, where so much of individual and social life and custom has been warped, twisted, spoiled by sin, the very struggle of a man to be good and just, to make the world a better place in which to live, may well bring down upon him additional suffering from the obtuseness and often enough from the malice of men.

Jesus' case is the extreme example of this sort of thing. Ultimately, in the intention of those leaders of the people who rejected him, it was because he was good and just and preached goodness and justice and tried to lead the entire people to their historic divine mission of perfect truth and justice that he had to be killed. And Jesus' case is extreme in another way, for here not only does the innocent one receive an evil and unjust lot, but he receives the worst lot one can think of — complete rejection, abandonment, failure, scorn, plus the most intense physical suffering. Everything about it seems the perversion of right order. The reader of the gospels cannot help but be shocked, scandalized, by the closing chapters of Jesus' life. True, there are the predictions of the passion ahead of time, but the disproportion between the beautiful, excellent, inspiring life, the noble figure presented in the first half of the gospels and the miserable end inflicted upon him in the last is simply too intense. Reason boggles.

He who hears the message and believes, accepts that history as God's salvation in this real world and as the way God chose for men to pass from subjection to sin to real life.

He likewise believes that this is God's act of salvation; that God has sent his dearly beloved Son to save us in this way;

that God himself has come to save us; that God was in Christ reconciling the world to himself; that by this do we know God's love for us.

And he believes finally that this is the conquest of sin and of death: not the mere undergoing of physical suffering and death, but the doing what Jesus did — accepting them when they are willed by God as a way to offset the malice of sin, accepting them out of submission and obedience to God our loving Father, with confidence that God is working out through them our own greater good; accepting them out of love for our fellowmen, in order to share their lot and in order to render their lot easier and more bearable. He believes that, suffering in this spirit, Jesus has overcome sin and death, and that because he did precisely this God has raised him and has given him "a name above all names, so that at the name of Jesus everyone in heaven, on earth, and beneath the earth should bend the knee and should publicly acknowledge to the glory of God the Father that JESUS, CHRIST IS LORD" (Phil 2, 9–11).

This is his belief in the objective historical fact that the message recounts. And he believes in regard to that fact that one who accepts these principles in his own life must aim at the good and holy service of God as Jesus did and accept the unjust suffering that comes to him because of it as Jesus did and because Jesus did, in the power of the Spirit of Jesus, which faith and baptism have conferred upon him. He further believes that such a one will come to resurrection and life and glorification too, with and because of Jesus.

For me too, he believes, sin and suffering and death are conquered if I voluntarily link myself with Christ by faith and baptism and if I persevere in the sentiments God thereupon and thereby infuses into me in his Spirit.

But if faith brings man to this view and to this share in the Spirit and in the dispositions of Jesus, then all of life takes on another color and meaning. Then suffering is not a penalty and can be a joy. He can welcome it when it comes, remembering that it is working for him in Christ a hundredweight of glory, that it is producing in him the image of Christ, firstborn among many brethren. Suffering, persecution, death can be seen as blessings, as deeper and fuller shares in the reality of Christ's redemptive cross. Especially when the suffering and persecution and death come from the effort to accomplish positive good, to preach the gospel, to save and help others, then one is that much more like Christ.

But even when it comes by accident, from natural events, from human ignorance, from one's own sins, it can be accepted and transformed, redeemed, in union with Christ.

Persecution and martyrdom are the supreme manifestations of this principle for the Christian, for they approach the closest of all to the salvific reality of Christ. But the New Testament realistically and practically goes on to point out all the ramifications of the same idea through the whole of the Christian life. The cross and the certainty of resurrection through faithful acceptance become the foundation for all sorts of exhortations to necessary virtues. These virtues together make up a single group which receives a special emphasis, and, indeed, needs special emphasis because of the special difficulties connected with it.

After the model of Christ's faithful suffering and in hope of the same resurrection the epistle to the Hebrews calls for endurance, perseverance, patience, faith (in the sense of believing without wavering that God will bring all to a happy consummation, that God is really working out our good through these long trials). "Let us eagerly throw ourselves into the struggle before us, and persevere, with our gaze fixed on Jesus, the pioneer and perfect embodiment of faith. He, in view of the joy offered him, underwent crucifixion with contempt of its disgrace, and has taken his seat at the right hand of God's throne. Meditate on him who in his own person endured such great opposition at the hands of sinners; then your souls will not be overwhelmed with discouragement. Your resistance in the struggle against sin has not yet gone as far as bloodshed" (Heb 12, 2–4).

"Submission" and "obedience" are other key words which ring changes on the same theme. Christ's act of salvation was obedient and submissive bearing of the cross: "Be submissive to every human authority for the Lord's sake" (1 Pt 2, 13).

Slaves should be subject and show their masters every mark of respect, not only those masters who are kind and considerate, but even those who are unreasonably exacting. In fact it is pleasing to God if, mindful of him, one endures the pain of unjust suffering. What glory is there if you patiently take a beating for having sinned? But to endure suffering for having done good earns a claim on God's favor. Really, you have been called to suffer, because Christ on his part suffered for you, leaving you his example that you might follow in his footsteps.

> "He committed no sin,
> and no deceit was found on his lips."

When he was insulted, he did not return the insult; when he was mistreated, he did not threaten, but entrusted himself to him who judges justly. He bore our sins in his own body on the cross that we, having died to our sins, might live for holiness (1 Pt 2, 18-24).

Render your service heartily and willingly in view of the fact that you are serving the Lord and not men . . . (Eph 6, 7).

Let everyone submit himself to the ruling authorities, for there exists no authority not ordained by God (Rom 13, 1).

Render to all men their due: tribute to whom tribute is due; taxes to whom taxes are due; respect to whom respect is due; honor to whom honor is due (Rom 13, 7).

. . . be subject to the presbyters. And all of you should clothe yourselves with humility in your mutual dealings. As you know,

> "God resists the proud
> but gives his grace to the humble."

Humble yourselves then under the mighty hand of God, that he may exalt you in due time. Cast all your anxiety on him, because he takes care of you (1 Pt 5, 5-7).

Remind the faithful to be subject to rulers and authorities, to be obedient to commands, to be ready for any good undertaking. Remind them to speak evil of no one, to avoid quarreling, to be considerate and show perfect gentleness to all men. For we ourselves were once without understanding, without obedience, deceived, slaves to various lusts and pleasures. We lived in malice and envy; we were hateful and hating one another. But when the goodness and kindness of God our Savior toward all mankind appeared, then, not because of deeds we ourselves had done in a state of holiness, but in virtue of his mercy, he saved us through the bath in which the Holy Spirit regenerates and renews us. This Spirit God has richly poured out on us through Jesus Christ our Savior, in order that, made holy by his grace, we may in hope become heirs of life everlasting (Ti 3, 1–7).

. . . Make every effort to supplement faith with moral courage, moral courage with knowledge, knowledge with self-control, self-control with patience, patience with piety, piety with brotherly affection, brotherly affection with love. If you have these virtues in abundance, they will make you both active and fruitful, and bring you to the deep knowledge of our Lord Jesus Christ (2 Pt 1, 5–8).

Thus obedience, submission, endurance, proof under trial, patience, meekness, humility, perseverance, faith, etc., make up a whole family of conclusions as to daily moral life, all flowing from the acceptance of the cross. Thus Paul can even write:

. . . Gladly, therefore, will I boast of my infirmities, that the power of Christ may spread a sheltering cover over me. For this reason I take delight, for Christ's sake, in infirmities, in insults, in hardships, in persecutions, in distresses. For when I am weak, then I am strong (2 Cor 12, 9–10).

We, the strong, ought to bear the infirmities of the weak, and not please ourselves. Let everyone of us please his neighbor, doing him good by edifying him, since Christ did not please himself, but, as it is written,
"The reproaches of those who reproach you
have fallen upon me."
For whatever has been written beforehand, has been written for our instruction, that through the patient endurance and consolation afforded by the Scriptures we may have hope. May then the God who imparts patience and comfort grant you this unity of sentiments among yourselves, according to Jesus Christ, that, one in spirit, you may in a harmonious chorus glorify the God and Father of our Lord Jesus Christ (Rom 15, 1–6).

CHAPTER 7

Love

BUT suffering, even joy in suffering, was not all of God's message in the cross and resurrection. It was not even the major part of it. What happened to Christ meant hope and strength in human trials for the believer. Christ's way of bearing it was the solution, the way to victory, over the evils all men have to bear. But his way was not one of simple endurance or even simple, but perfect, submission to the divine design. Christ's way was a way of love.

And so the other half of the divine pattern worked out in Christ for the salvation of those who believe is love.

> . . . God's love was made manifest among us by the fact that God sent his only begotten Son into the world that we might have life through him. . . . if God so loved us, we in turn ought to love one another (1 Jn 4, 9–11).

> No one can give a greater proof of his love than by laying down his life for his friends. You are my friends . . . (Jn 15, 13).

> . . . the Son of Man did not come into the world to be served, but to serve and to give his life as a ransom for many (Mk 10, 45).

> We know what love is from the fact that Jesus Christ laid down his life for us. We too ought to lay down our lives for our brothers (1 Jn 3, 16).

> The life that I now live, in this body, I live by faith in the Son of God, who loved me and sacrificed himself for me (Gal 2, 20).

While we were still helpless, Christ at the appointed time died for us wicked people. Why, it is only with difficulty that a person will die to save a good man. Yes, it is only for a worthy person that a man may, perhaps, have the courage to face death. But God proves his love for us, because, when we were still sinners, Christ died for us (Rom 5, 6–8).

The acceptance of God's word of salvation in the cross, the acceptance of the dying and rising Christ as our salvation, points the life of the Christian in the same direction of love. And when a man's act of acceptance is turned by God into true salvation through the gift of the Spirit, the Spirit comes to him for the same purpose; namely, that "the love of God is poured forth in our hearts by his Spirit who is given to us."

Thus the Christian does not merely die and rise with Christ. Christianity will not be a mere mystic stoicism. Christian lives, sufferings, abstinences, deaths — and resurrections — will be, must be, if they are to follow the great pattern laid down for them, done out of love.

And so love becomes all through the New Testament a central object of teaching. In explaining the nature of Christ's redemptive work, the apostles make it more and more clear that the love with which Christ acted, was, like his obedience, the supreme value in that which he did. He was not put to death as an animal victim might be, unknowing or even unwilling. And the excellence of his act is never sought in the peculiar extremity of his sufferings — no attempt is made to catalog them, to dwell on their intensity as in some later piety. It is the motive, the spirit, the attitude of Jesus in suffering which makes his work acceptable to God and effective for us. And that is a spirit of obedience and of love.

The believer, in the Spirit, is moved to practice the same love. If he believes that this which Jesus has done is his salvation, he sees and feels at once that to have that salvation completely, fully, in a way which will lead to the perfect consummation it reached in Christ, he himself must become part of that which Christ has done. He must enter into it, feel it, have it cut into his own life. "Be imitators of me, as I am of Christ," "that others may be imitators of you" as St. Paul writes again and again.

The Christian too wants to love, and love like that, if necessary, even unto death. Nor is it long before the new Christian community learns that the possibility of death's coming to seal and crown their acceptance of this way of life is not in any way remote.

And so love becomes central in New Testament preaching and writing. Every document mentions it, every one exhorts to it. And almost always, in one way or another, they add the important fact, learned from Jesus himself, that, in the last analysis, love is the one thing necessary, the great commandment. For instance:

. . . he who loves his neighbor has fulfilled the Law. For the commandments . . . all are summed up in this saying, "You shall love your neighbor as yourself." . . . Love, therefore, is the complete fulfilment of the Law (Rom 13, 9–10).

So we now have these three, faith, hope, and love, but the greatest of them is love (1 Cor 13, 13).

. . . in love serve one another. Why, the whole Law is fulfilled by the observance of the one precept: "You shall love your neighbor as yourself" (Gal 5, 13–14).

But over all these other virtues clothe yourselves with love; it is the bond that perfects and binds them together (Col 3, 14).

. . . the royal law, which according to the Scriptures reads, "Love your neighbor as yourself . . ." (Jas 2, 8).

Above all things practice constant love among yourselves; it wins forgiveness for many sins (1 Pt 4, 8).

This is precisely the message which you have heard from the beginning — that we should love one another (1 Jn 3, 11).

The commandment, as you have heard from the beginning, is that you make love the rule of your life (2 Jn 6).

This point is so obvious that it has given rise to certain errors of interpretation. Thus some have said that love is the one central theme of the New Testament, overlooking the fact that love is part of a larger theme — Christ's death and resurrection and our

chance to share in it. Others have said that at least love is the
one essential element in the original preaching of Jesus — a simple
religion of the Fatherhood of God and the brotherhood of man.
And they add sometimes that this is the great new element in
Christianity as over against Judaism.

But this too is exaggerated. Jesus preached love, yes, but so did
the prophets. And that the law could be summed up in love, the
author of Deuteronomy knew very well, and the best of the rabbis
did not forget it. Finally, to make the one distinctive element of
Christianity precisely that element which the greatest founders of
other religions and the best moral philosophers of all times have
presented as their teaching, too, is to run the risk of reducing
Christianity to the same level as these others and perhaps to take
away its significance as real revelation completely.

For there is a sense in which the ideal of love is an obvious
one. "Let us love one another." How simple and, to any thinking
man, how clearly desirable and even necessary. Of course if all
men loved one another, the world would be a better place, a
veritable heaven. State the ideal simply, as for example, in the
Golden Rule, and it has an instant appeal for human nature. Why
should men fight, strive with one another? Why should they harm
and cheat and lie? There is abundance aplenty on the earth. Let
us use it for the greatest good of all.

If every man treated all other men, singly and collectively,
as he himself would wish to be treated, of course life would be
easy and beautiful, human relations unsnarled. Nine tenths of
the evil in the world would disappear at once, and what was
left — the portion of pain, suffering, evil resulting from purely
natural causes like disease, storm, earthquake — could be reduced
tremendously in a short time if all human ingenuity and effort
were concentrated on that goal.

Idealists and, with increasing frequency today, even statesmen
speak up to say it is not reasonable that the world should go on
putting so much time, effort, and money into producing the means
of destruction and death. The same expenditures, the same dedication to work and research, could be turned to producing and

distributing the means of life, and could banish want and misery from the world.

The same ideal lies behind the appeals which even communism directs to the poor and miserable. Why not set up a society, the early communists dreamed, in which all would strive with all their might for the greater good of all, instead of fighting for individual gain and profit to the possible hurt of their fellowmen? From each according to his ability; to each according to his needs! How simple! How beautiful! The ideal is instantly appealing. And since it was first formulated, many have been willing to fight and die for it. The trouble is that as they find out in practice how little capable ordinary human nature is of living up to that ideal, devoted communists have also been willing to kill for it.

The love of the New Testament is not a beautiful ideal for a far-distant future. Or rather, it is not only that. As a picture of a perfect human society, it does remain for the most part an ideal toward which we all strive. That ideal will become full reality only when all men have accepted and are practicing the new life in Christ. But as a challenge and a program for the individual here and now, New Testament love is quite a different thing. For it does not say: "Let us love one another some day." Or: "How nice it would be if we loved one another." Anyone can say that. The New Testament says and means: "Let us love one another *now*." That is, right now, when our love may, as a matter of fact, find no response whatsoever on the side of its object; when our love may just possibly arouse only contempt, pity, hatred. Let us love in spite of all that. Let us love our enemies, let us love those who hate us and persecute us, especially if they persecute us because we love them.

This is quite a different thing. This formula and demand for love takes into account the simple fact that we are living in a world which is not by any means ideal, a world where men in general do not live, think, and act according to the principle of love. In a world where everyone else loved us, it would be perhaps easy to love like the rest, and love in return. That would be paradise, and, according to Christian revelation, that was God's

original plan for mankind. It would have existed and lasted forever if men had not, beginning with the very first man, freely
chosen to reject that plan and turn to selfishness and sin.

But we do live in this world of sin. It is a world in which men
often act selfishly, oppose one another, exploit one another when
they can, remove one another when they find their fellows an
obstacle between themselves and their desired goals. We do the
same ourselves.

In such a world the New Testament proposes that the believer
should go forth and love. In this real world, the man attempting
to practice such love without reserve is sure to meet exploitation,
pain, suffering, resentment, persecution. The New Testament principle recognizes this. And thus what appears at first sight to be
the most idealistic of its teachings on love, turns out to be the
most realistic of all: "Love your enemies," it says. "Pray for those
who persecute and calumniate you."

But this deeper and more accurate approach is not so likely
to make an instant appeal or find an immediate and automatic
response in the hearts of men, not to mention in their lives and
in their actions. That is perhaps why this challenge, this program,
was not made primarily in words. Much more than words were
needed. It had to be lived. And it had to be communicated on a
person-to-person basis, from heart to heart, from life to life, so
that it could touch and draw upon the deepest resources of the
human personality. And so "the Word became man and lived
among us" (Jn 1, 14), and "We know what love is from the fact
that Jesus Christ laid down his life for us" (1 Jn 3, 16). And now:
"A new commandment I give you: love one another as I have
loved you" (Jn 13, 34).

But most important of all, and distinguishing the Christian
message from all others, is this: it does not merely sketch the
ideal; it makes the ideal possible in practice. The New Testament
not only admits that men are of themselves incapable of living
up to such high norms of action; it positively teaches that
they are incapable. The perfect love is always presented as love
given freely by God through the Holy Spirit. It comes to men

as a share in Christ's love — which is a share in the love and the life of God himself. "Love takes its origin in God, and everyone that loves is a child of God" (1 Jn 4, 7); "if we love one another, God abides in us and his love in us reaches perfection. We know that we abide in him and he in us by the fact that he has made us partakers of his Spirit" (1 Jn 4, 12–14). "We know and believe in God's enduring love at work among us. God is love, and he who abides in love, abides in God and God in him" (1 Jn 4, 16).

Those who believed and were baptized, found in practice that they could live up to the high call of love, in the Spirit. Thus: "All the believers were united, and held all things in common. They would sell their possessions and goods and distribute them to everyone as need required. Daily with one accord they attended the temple, and, breaking bread at their homes, took their food with gladness and simplicity of heart, praising God and having the good will of all the people" (Acts 2, 44–47). And "They . . . continued to enjoy great popularity. No one among the faithful was in want" (Acts 4, 32–34).

"See how they love one another."

And so too out of the love which God gave them grew the Christian community, one in love, one in union with Christ. That community we shall study further in Chapter 9. It is the same community which has attempted through the centuries to grow up to the fullness of Christ in the bond and union of love supplied by the Holy Spirit; the same community in which in every generation have arisen saints who put such love into practice in a way that astounded the eyes of men. And in that same community countless others in every generation have had the experience that they too could live lives at least approaching that perfection, if they only perseveringly put to use the means which their faith actually placed at their disposal.

❖   ❖   ❖

Thus we see on the one hand suffering, patience, and submission, in union with our Lord, who became obedient unto death, even the death of the cross; and on the other, love — effective, real love that shows itself in real works of love, kindness, goodness toward all men, even to the point of complete self-sacrifice, as Jesus "loved us and sacrificed himself for us." These are the key virtues that stem immediately from that act by which the Christian really believes that this suffering, dying man is the Christ, is God's salvation for us, is the Son of God come to make it possible for us to share in a glorious resurrection like his own.

Thus, often enough, patience and love appear together as a summary of the Christian life: "Sound in faith, love, and patience" (Ti 2, 2); "Pursue holiness, piety, faith, love, patience, mildness" (1 Tm 6, 11). Paul can exhort his disciple to follow "my doctrine, my conduct, my purpose: my faith, my long-suffering, my love, and my patience" (2 Tm 3, 10). The great exhortation of Philippians is built on them:

> Only let your lives be worthy of the gospel of Christ, so that whether I come and see you or am absent, I may hear that you stand with unity of mind and heart, fighting together to maintain the faith of the gospel. Do not be terrified in any way by your adversaries. Your steadfastness, a gift of God, is a sign to them of their destruction, but to you of your salvation. For you have been given the favor on Christ's behalf, not only of having faith in him but also of suffering for him. Your struggle is the same as mine. You formerly saw me engaged in it, and now hear how I continue that struggle. If, therefore, you would give me any comfort in Christ and any encouragement such as love imparts, if you have any spiritual communion with me, and if you would show me some affection and compassion, make my joy complete by unanimity of sentiments and of love springing from one soul and a unity of thought. Never act out of rivalry or vainglory, but in humility deem others as better than yourselves. Look not to your personal interests, but rather to those of others. Be of the same mind as Christ Jesus, who, though he is by nature God, did not consider his equality with God a condition to be clung to, but emptied himself by taking the nature of a slave, fashioned as he was to the likeness of men and recognized by outward appearance as man. He humbled himself and became obedient to death; yes, to death on a cross. This is why God has exalted him . . . (Phil 1, 27–2, 9).

This is the point of Ephesians: "I . . . exhort you to conduct yourselves in a manner worthy of the calling to which you have been called, with all humility and meekness. Have patience and bear lovingly with one another. Strive anxiously to preserve harmony of mind by means of the bond which effects peace" (Eph 4, 1–3).

The first epistle of St. Peter exhorts over and over that all Christians be submissive, be subject, bear suffering and evil after the example of Christ, and concludes the exhortation with the general call to "be like-minded, sympathetic, brotherly in affection, full of mercy, humble. Do not return evil for evil or insult for insult; on the contrary, bless, because you have been called to inherit a blessing" (1 Pt 3, 8–9) and "above all things practice constant love among yourselves; it wins forgiveness for many sins. Show ungrudging hospitality to one another. Each of you should use what endowments he has received in the service of others, as good stewards of the manifold bounty of God" (1 Pt 4, 8–10).

> Let love be without pretense. Hate what is evil; cling to what is good. Love one another with fraternal charity, anticipating one another with honor. Do not be slothful in zeal, be fervent in spirit; it is the Lord you serve. Rejoice in hope. Be patient in tribulation, persevering in prayer. Relieve the needs of the saints, exercise hospitality with eagerness. Bless those who persecute you; bless and do not curse. Rejoice with those who rejoice, weep with those who weep. Agree in thought with one another, aspiring not to high things, but agreeing in thought with lowly people. Be not wise in your own eyes. To no man render evil for evil, but take thought for decent conduct in the sight of all men. If it be possible, as far as lies in your power, be at peace with all men. Do not avenge yourselves. . . . Be not conquered by evil, but conquer evil by good (Rom 12, 9–19, 21).

This passage, centering on the Christian virtues of patient submission and love, is followed by a short exhortation to submission to ruling authorities (13, 1–7) and then by

> Let there be no unpaid debt except the debt of mutual love, because he who loves his neighbor has fulfilled the Law. For the commandments:
> "You shall not commit adultery;
> you shall not kill;

you shall not steal;
you shall not covet";
and if there is any other commandment, all are summed up in the saying:

"You shall love your neighbor as yourself."

Love does no evil to a neighbor. Love, therefore, is the complete fulfillment of the Law (13, 8–10).

The second letter to the Corinthians is built around the theme of the apostolate, the work Paul does for Christ as preacher. And over and over in that letter, he explains the sufferings he has borne for them, just as Christ suffered for love of us, and he exhorts his readers to follow his example: "As the sufferings which we have to endure for Christ's sake are superabundant, so is the comfort we receive through Christ superabundant. If we are afflicted, it is to comfort and save you. If we are comforted, it is to bring you comfort. It does its work when you endure the selfsame sufferings as we" (1, 5–6).

Those same basic virtues are unfolded into the list called the "fruits of the Spirit": " . . . love, joy, peace, long-suffering, affability, goodness, fidelity, gentleness, self-control" (Gal 5, 22). This complex of virtues, under slightly varying names, has the place of honor in all the epistles.

CHAPTER 8

Endurance vs. Love

BEGINNING even before the time of Celsus and continuing past Nietzsche to the present, theoretical attacks on Christianity have often centered on the practical message of the cross. Christianity, according to one version of such attacks, is a religion for weaklings. People who cannot or dare not try to change an evil situation in which they find themselves, make a virtue out of submission, patience, quiet and humble acceptance. Christianity, they say, is a religion of slaves. Those who find themselves in a bad situation glorify their own lot and find comfort and strength enough in the imaginary good of sharing in the cross.

Christianity, say some, is a religion for the exploiting classes, designed to keep quiet, obedient, and humble the long exploited. Christianity, say some, is essentially an enemy of progress and of the human race. For all the good that mankind has achieved has been achieved precisely as a result of discontent. Man is distinguished from the animals precisely in his ability to analyze a complex situation, envision a better future, and then work toward that better goal. The doctrine of patience, submission, acceptance of the cross, if widely accepted and practiced, would make progress impossible.

All of these are far from having heard or understood the message of the cross. But since such deep misunderstanding is possible and even frequent, it seems worthwhile to sum up once again what we have said about the submission and patience aspects of the doctrine of the cross in the explicit light of what we have seen about the cross as message of love. For the essential error in all the attacks listed above is threefold: first, they do not accept the reality of the resurrection, either as past event or as promise. Ultimately of course this means simply that they do not believe. But it does not help them to understand the message of the New Testament.

Second, they take into consideration no more than half of the New Testament doctrine on the cross and the Christian's call to share it. That is, they see the part that calls for patience, submission, obedience, suffering. They neglect the part that makes of the cross a call to love.

Third, they overlook (quite irrationally for a scientific observer) the principle once formulated by St. Augustine: One must interpret the New Testament in the light of the New Testament, and New Testament teaching in the light of New Testament practice.

We shall not argue with them as regards the first point. That is a matter every man must decide for himself. The evidence for our belief they know. But we shall try, in conformity with the third point, the general principle of interpretation, to review typical instances of how the New Testament presents the practice of the doctrine of the cross, and we shall then take another look at its theoretical teaching on this doctrine in the light of those examples.

First of all, the principle of interpretation itself which we shall try to follow is a principle of common sense. Interpret the teachings of the New Testament by the actions of the New Testament. This means of course the actions which the same New Testament relates as being done by the community itself and by its leaders, not by the enemies of the faith. It would mean too, of course, those actions which are either praised or at least presented as typical and normal, not those which are criticized or reprobated.

Why is it a simple principle of common sense? Because, as we have been saying all along, the New Testament was written under the direction and with the approbation of the community and its leaders. They are the ones who recognized and preserved the New Testament writings as God's word. The New Testament cannot then be teaching something which is in complete contradiction to what they are practicing. For the very life of that community was an attempt to live out God's word in practice. And God's written word in the New Testament reflects the life of precisely that community as a pattern for the Church in future ages. Our principle is, in other words, the same one which the classical critics use when they find the New Testament recording Jesus' command to baptize in the name of the Father, Son, and Holy Spirit, and at the same time recording again and again in Acts that the Christians were baptizing "in the name of Jesus." Either the formulas can be reconciled, or one is a later addition to the text. But a patent contradiction between recorded doctrine and recorded action is simply impossible.

Now, in regard to our present problem, what do we find? The community was preaching and teaching joy in suffering, but when certain "widows were being neglected in the daily distribution of alms," they appoint deacons to see that everyone gets a fair share (Acts 6). When a great persecution breaks out against the Church in Jerusalem, "all except the apostles were scattered abroad throughout the land of Judea and Samaria" (Chap. 8). When the "Greek-speaking Jews sought to kill him," the brethren brought St. Paul down to Caesarea and sent him on to Tarsus (9, 30). When a great famine was foretold, "the disciples, each according to his means, determined to send relief to the brothers dwelling in Judea" (11, 29). When Peter was imprisoned by Herod, "fervent prayer was being offered to God for him by the Church" (12, 5), and when, in answer to these prayers, Peter was delivered from prison by an angel, "they were beside themselves with joy" and Peter "departed and went to another place" (12, 17).

When certain Jews stirred up a persecution against Paul and Barnabas, the latter "shook the dust from their feet in protest and went to Iconium" (13, 51). The same thing happened at Iconium (Chap. 14). Paul defended himself before the court in Chapter 18, as he did later several times more. In Chapter 20, when Eutychus falls from a third-story window and is picked up dead, Paul tells the community: "Do not be alarmed; life is still in him," and after he has brought him back to life, they were "not a little comforted."

They preached not to resist evil, according to the Sermon on the Mount, but when "Elymas the magician opposed them, trying to turn the proconsul away from the faith," Paul looked him in the eye and said, "You thoroughgoing scoundrel and deceiver, son of the devil, enemy of all that is holy, will you never stop trying to make crooked the straight ways of the Lord?" And he struck the man blind (13, 4–12).

When they had arrested Paul, in Chapter 22, and "had stretched him out for the scourges," he appealed to his Roman citizenship, and "at once, therefore, those who were about to torture him drew back from him. Even the tribune was alarmed to find that Paul was a Roman citizen and because he had bound him" (22, 28–29).

When Paul knew that the Jews had laid an ambush for him, he saw to it that word of this got to the tribune so that he was protected by "two hundred soldiers, seventy cavalry, and two hundred spearmen" (23, 23–24).

They preached that Christians should be submissive and obedient to lawfully constituted authority. But when the Jewish authorities ordered them to cease their work, they answered that "We ought to obey God rather than men" and continued as they had been doing. They were to take no thought for the morrow, but large parts of some of the Pauline letters are devoted to his plans for his travels and future work, organization of his churches for the future, arranging collections of material goods, money and food, as alms for the poor and famine-stricken. They healed the sick and raised the dead, not only as signs to the world, but within their own believing communities for the comfort of body and soul. And Paul writes: "He that will not work, neither let him eat," and "live quietly, laboring with your hands," and "a man who cannot take good care of his own household, how can he be a bishop, taking charge of God's Church?" and "take a little wine for your stomach's sake."

How can all these things be reconciled with the doctrine of the cross, of patient suffering of evil, of other-worldly detachment from success, prosperity, material well-being here below?

To make the case even stronger, consider the example of Christ himself. He slipped out of his enemies' hands again and again when "his hour was not yet come." He attacked them fiercely for their errors and their corruption, thus resisting vigorously the greatest evil, moral evil and corruption in high places, and thus giving an example of resistance to established authority that not all critics of Christianity would dare to follow. He relieved pains of body and soul, "having compassion on the multitude." He challenged the man who struck him on one cheek when he stood before the high priest, as did St. Paul in his trial in Acts 23: "You whitewashed wall!" he said. "Do you sit there to try me according to the Law, and in violation of the Law order me to be struck?"

Does this simply mean that no one, not even Jesus himself, observed the moral standards which necessarily follow as conclusions from the gospel? Not at all. It means that we have not yet understood the entire message. For we saw earlier that the cross is not only a message of accepting the hard things which Divine Providence sends. It is also a message of love. It is God's love for us, when we were yet sinners, and it demands our love for one another. "A new commandment I give unto you, that you love one another as I have loved you." "If he has loved us, we also ought to love one another."

And in what does this love consist? "We must love not in word but in deed."

> Religious practice pure and undefiled before God our Father is this: to care for orphans and widows in their affliction . . . (Jas 1, 27).

> If a brother or sister has no clothes or daily food, and one of you says to them, "Go, and be at peace; warm yourselves and eat plenty," yet does not give them the things that are necessary for the body, of what good is it? (Jas 2, 15–16.)

> We know what love is from the fact that Jesus Christ laid down his life for us. We too ought to lay down our lives for our brothers. How then can the love of God abide in him who possesses worldly goods, and seeing his brother in need, closes

his heart to him? Little children, let us not love merely in word or with the tongue, but in action, in reality (1 Jn 3, 16–18).

Relieve the needs of the saints, exercise hospitality . . . (Rom 12, 13).

Paul, writing to the people of Corinth about the collection he is taking up for the church in Jerusalem, says: ". . . you should excel in this work of charity. I am not speaking by way of command, but to test the genuineness of your love, by means of your eagerness to help others" (2 Cor 8, 7–8).

As the climactic Last Judgment scene in the gospel of Matthew makes clear, so compelling is this obligation of love that the final salvation or damnation of all men will depend precisely upon it — upon practical, really exercised love in deed:

"When the Son of Man returns in his glory, and escorted by all the angels, he will seat himself on a throne befitting his glory. All the nations will assemble in his presence, and he will part mankind into two groups just as a shepherd parts the sheep from the goats. The sheep he will range at his right, and the goats at his left.

"Then the king will say to those at his right: 'Welcome, favored of my Father! Take possession of the kingdom prepared for you from the beginning of the world. For when I was hungry, you gave me to eat; when I was thirsty, you gave to me drink; when I was a stranger, you took me into your homes; when I was naked, you covered me; when I was sick, you visited me; when I was in prison, you came to see me. . . . inasmuch as you did this to one of these least brethren of mine, you did it to me.'

"Next he will say to those at his left: 'Out of my sight, you cursed ones! Off into the everlasting fire prepared for the devil and his ministers! For when I was hungry, you did not give me to eat; when I was thirsty, you did not give me to drink; when I was a stranger, you did not take me into your homes; when naked, you did not cover me; when sick and in prison, you did not visit me. . . . insofar as you failed to render these services to one of those least ones, you also failed to render them to me.' And so the latter will be consigned to everlasting punishment, while the saints will enter into everlasting life" (Mt 25, 31–46).

The point is clear. The message, the command of love, is so fundamental, that salvation itself will depend on whether or not one made sincere efforts, labored sincerely, gave generously of himself and what he has, to spare others the pains of cold, hunger, thirst, sickness, prison. Salvation depends on working to alleviate those pains which are the necessary accompaniment of poverty: homelessness, hunger, thirst. He who will be saved must combat those things which are the necessary result of man's inhumanity to man: the sad lot of the prisoner, the results of man's imperfect control over the forces of nature: the lonely and miserable sickbed.

And yet "Blessed are you, the poor, for yours is the kingdom of God. Blessed are you who now go hungry, for you shall have your fill. . . . On the other hand, utterly wretched are you, the rich, for you have your comfort here and now. Utterly wretched are you who now have your fill of everything" (Lk 6, 20–25).

How then are these teachings to be reconciled? We must reconcile them in theory as the New Testament shows the first-generation Christians reconciling them in practice. That is, love comes first. "This above all, love one another." "The greatest of these is charity." Love is the most important; and love alone is the wellspring, fountainhead of action. They do not go about seeking opportunities to suffer, fail, submit themselves. They do go about seeking opportunities to help their fellows — first of all, in preaching the truth, the good news; second, in doing good "and winning favor with all the people." "Heal the sick, raise the dead, cast out devils" (Mt 10, 8). Their deeds and their preaching do tend to make the world a better place in which to live, human society more viable, life more tolerable. They do combat evil, and sin is evil, suffering is evil, sickness and death are evil. If they had perfect success, if all men gave up "what is morally disgraceful, dishonesty, wickedness, greed, ill-will, envy, murderous intent, strife, deceit, rancor," etc. (Rom 1) and concentrated instead on using all energies to the full for bettering the material, intellectual, and moral state of all their fellowmen, there is no doubt that most of the world's problems would be solved. Life would be so close to paradise, we would almost have the kingdom of heaven here.

That then is the Christian "program" — a building up in love: an honest, sincere, dedicated service of one's fellowmen; doing the best one knows how to see to it that no one is hungry, thirsty, shelterless, abandoned to disease, to languishing in prison, etc., as well as "teaching, exhorting, reproving," and all the rest too.

But that is not the whole story. The gospel message is more practical than that. There will be difficulties, obstacles, and lack of success. "The poor you have always with you" (Mt 26, 11). Moreover, every man's sin, anywhere in the world, tends to do its part to corrupt the social fabric. Every act of selfishness, cruelty, injustice, unbridled lust, does harm not only to a man's immediate associates, but makes it to some degree harder for the entire social structure to function as it should and ideally could. And, of course, no matter how long or how well the apostles preach, every man remains free and must make his own decision as to how far he will cooperate. Therefore, no amount of effort is going to do away with all the evil in the world. There will be goats left to stand on the King's left hand when he lines up the nations for judgment.

Moreover "all who want to live piously in Christ Jesus will suffer persecutions" (2 Tm 3, 12). "You will be handed over to courts of justice, and flogged in synagogues, and confronted with governors and kings for my sake" (Mk 13, 9). As recounted already in the Old Testament book of the Wisdom of Solomon, the wicked, seeing the just man's ways, will feel offended by them and say: "Come, let us try him with violence and persecution and see if he will remain faithful. . . ." Besides, simply speaking practically, it is obvious that all attempts to introduce more just, humane ways of living among large numbers of men, and any efforts to relieve the condition of large numbers of the poor and distressed, are going to conflict with what some people somewhere consider their own vested interests.

Beyond that there is another trial connected with the program. The servant, even the originally faithful one, is likely to say, "My master is long in coming" and, finding the strain of long and apparently uncompensated observance too much, "will begin to beat his fellow servants and carouse" (Mt 24, 43–51) etc. Perseverance in well-doing is no easy test.

Add all these considerations together and one sees the point at which comes into play all the teaching about the necessity of suffering as the way of salvation. The necessary consequences of one's own failures and sins as well as the failures and sins of others add up to a great load of difficulty, pain, and suffering to bear. Then comes into play the true example of Jesus, who continued the life he was living, the teaching he was doing, to which God called him and for which he had sent him, even though he knew and saw clearly the consequences to which it all would lead. He knew the consummation ahead of him. The gospels are full of accounts of his growing conflicts with the authorities who would eventually destroy him on the cross. But as Christianity's message is not one of weakness but of strength, he continued his work.

So did the Christians after him. They do what must be done, what "the love of Christ urges" them to do. And when they, occupied in obeying God rather than men, find — as they must — the cross in what they do, then "Blessed are you when you are reviled, or persecuted, or made a target for nothing but malicious lies — for my sake. Be joyful — leap for joy" (Mt 5, 11). "For Christ too suffered for us, the just for the unjust . . ." (1 Pt 3, 18). They rejoice to be able to say "with Christ I am nailed to the cross" (Gal 2, 19). And yet, they have not nailed themselves to that cross any more than Christ had nailed himself to his. They, as he, did always the will of God, and, in a sinful universe — sinful by the free choice of men, not by God's doing — such a life leads inevitably to the cross.

Thus, as we saw above, when the Church is persecuted, its members flee, are scattered, hide. When caught, they try to avoid the unjust punishments scheduled for them, insofar as this is possible without compromising the truth for which they stand — like St. Paul's appeal against being scourged. But when in the end they *are* scourged unjustly for Christ, when the evil has come upon them after all, then "they departed from the presence of the Sanhedrin, rejoicing that they had been counted worthy to suffer disgrace for the name of Jesus" (Acts 5, 41). St. Paul can look back with affection on all that he has suffered as an apostle – the same things which he had tried to avoid by every rational means, short of giving up that apostolate: "fatiguing labors more abundant, imprisonments more frequent, lashings innumerable, many threats of death. From the Jews five times I received forty lashes less one. Three times I was scourged, once I was stoned, three times I suffered shipwreck; a night and a day I was adrift on the high sea," etc. (2 Cor 11, 23 ff.). And again: "We reflect credit on ourselves in all circumstances, as befits God's ministers – in great endurance, in afflictions, in hardships, in straits; in scourgings, in imprisonments, in riots, in fatigues, in sleepless nights, in fastings . . ." (2 Cor 6, 4–6).

There is a further point to be considered beyond all the above. We have been listing some unpleasant consequences of attempting to carry out the Christian program of love in practice. But there is also a good deal of sacrifice intrinsic to the program itself. That is, generosity to others implies of course giving up something oneself. Work for others implies labor and fatigue taken upon oneself. The Christian program for the building up of the world and of human society in love does call for the elimination of personal motives of gain and of aggrandizement. The motive force in the growth and perfection of society and the looking after the training and support of those who need it and the improving of civilization for the greater good of the greater number is always generous, and – if necessary – self-sacrificing love.

Those who think the New Testament ideal would not help to the building up of a better world – better and far more livable than the one we enjoy at present – presuppose that selfishness and gain are the only effective motive forces in great human enterprises. But they know nothing of the "power of the gospel" or of the "love which is poured forth in our hearts by the Holy Spirit who has been given us" (Rom 5, 5).

The New Testament ideal does not make the mistake of secular utopians, Marx for instance, with their conviction that somehow man himself, alone and unaided, can successfully build a society where every member is more devoted to the general good than to his own individual gain. The New Testament says rather no, this is impossible to man as he is. The necessary change in the basic structure of man's way of acting, in his basic motivations and habits, can and does come only in life in the Spirit of Christ. It is a gift of God. But a gift one receives through faith in Christ.

*   *   *

Doing good and bearing up under evil sum up the whole moral life. Love in act fulfills the first of these, patient endurance the second. In constantly returning to these two themes, the writers of the New Testament show how all human perfection flows from faith in Christ as our salvation.

Nevertheless, exhortations to specific virtues besides these also occur in the epistles. Sometimes there are whole lists of virtues, which modern research indicates have often been taken over from older Jewish moral exhortations. The main difference is that the Jewish exhortations had been based on the recollection of God's mighty work in the Exodus and on the pledge the individual had made to keep God's law as a member of the chosen people on the day he had been incorporated into the people by circumcision. The Christian exhortations were based on the recollection of God's mighty work in Christ and on the reminder that the Christian had in baptism voluntarily incorporated himself into Christ and Christ's death and resurrection. For instance: "The death that he died was a death to sin once for all, but the life that he lives is a life for God. Thus you too must consider yourselves dead to sin, but alive to God in Christ Jesus. Do not then let sin reign in your mortal body so as to obey its lusts. And do not go on offering your members to sin as instruments of iniquity, but once for all dedicate yourselves to God as men that have come to life from the dead, and your members as instruments of holiness for God" (Rom 6, 10–13).

Among such lists of virtues, two groups which recur with special frequency are warnings against unchastity of all sorts and warnings against "covetousness, which is idolatry."

Sometimes the exhortations are largely counsels of common

decency and good sense, like the demand that a bishop be "not a drinker or brawler, but considerate, not quarrelsome, not avaricious. He should manage well his own household, keeping his children under control and perfectly respectful. For if a man cannot manage his household, how can he take care of one of God's congregations?" (1 Tm 3, 3-5.)

Sometimes one or the other virtue or Christian right practice is explained at considerable length, as, for example, the treatment on chastity, virginity, marriage, and some opposite vices in 1 Corinthians, 5-7. In these cases there is usually a special problem of a particular community behind the exhortation. This is seen in the warnings to the people of Thessalonica against idleness (especially in 2 Thessalonians, 3, 6-15), the warnings against community strife which run through the two letters to the Corinthians, and the lesson on dietary observance to the mixed community at Rome.

These are, whenever possible, tied in directly with the basic Christian teaching. Chastity, for instance, is demanded by our union with Christ:

> The body is not for immorality but for the Lord, and the Lord is for the body. Just as God raised the Lord, so he will raise us by his power. Are you not aware that your bodies are members of Christ's body? Shall I then take the members of Christ and make them members of a prostitute? Never! Are you not aware that he who unites himself to a prostitute becomes one body with her? So says the Scripture, "The two shall become one flesh." But he who unites himself to the Lord, forms one spirit with him. Shun immorality. Every other sin a man may commit is outside the body, but the fornicator sins against his own body. Are you not aware that your body is the temple of the Holy Spirit? Him you have received from God! You are not your own masters. You have been bought, and at a price! So then, glorify the God in your body" (1 Cor 6, 13-20).

Factionalism is reprobated because we are one body in Christ (1 Cor 12). And, as to differences on observance in the matter of foods eaten:

> . . . he who eats does so for the Lord's sake, since he gives

thanks to the Lord. So too he who does not eat, abstains for the Lord's sake and gives thanks to God. None of us lives for himself and none dies for himself. If we live, we live for the Lord, and if we die, we die for the Lord. Whether we live or whether we die, we are the Lord's. To this end Christ died and lived, that he might be Lord both of the dead and of the living. But you, why do you condemn your brother? . . . Do not with what you eat destroy him for whom Christ died. . . . the kingdom of God does not consist in food and drink, but in holiness and peace and joy in the Holy Spirit . . . (Rom 14, 6–17).

Finally, a few individual virtues of an especially Christian tone recur with very great frequency. Joy, for instance, we have seen as part of the conquest of suffering and persecution, as well as a fruit of the Spirit. It is also a frequent subject of exhortation. The motives are obvious: the great gifts God has given us, the love God has shown and shows us, the future glory God has prepared for us. "Rejoice in the Lord always; . . . The Lord is near" (Phil 4, 4).

Prayer in the Spirit is always joined to exhortations to personal effort, because all we have and hope for is a gift of God.

Thanksgiving recurs constantly. Most of the epistles begin with a long prayer of thanks to God for the blessings he has poured out on his people. And in the exhortations themselves, thanksgiving and prayer and joy often appear together and closely linked. Finally the very name for their greatest prayer, the action which was the high point of their union with one another, their incorporation into Christ, and their self-oblation to God with him, was "Eucharist"; that is to say, "thanksgiving."

CHAPTER 9

The Church and the Eucharist

THOSE who accepted the gospel by believing and being baptized, received the gift of Christ's Spirit. This Spirit, they found, worked both in the individuals and in the whole community as a Spirit of love. He created in them a continual force and urgency toward union with others who had given themselves to the same gospel. And he formed them into the image of the Christ in whom they had believed and to whom they had given their allegiance —the Crucified and Risen.

The Spirit too gave this unity in another way, as we have also seen, by structuring the community. Not only that he "gave some to be apostles, some prophets, some teachers." He made his influence felt even in the choice of individual missions and the persons to fulfill them: "The Holy Spirit said: 'Set apart immediately for me Saul and Barnabas for the work to which I have called them.' . . . So, sent forth by the Holy Spirit, they went down to Seleucia . . ." (Acts 13, 2–4). "They passed through Phrygia and the Galatian country, because they had been forbidden by the Holy Spirit to speak the word in the province of Asia. When they came to the frontier of Mysia, they tried to enter Bithynia, but the Spirit of Jesus did not permit them" (Acts 16, 6–7). "The Spirit said to Philip: 'Go and stay near this carriage,'" (Acts 8, 29). "The Spirit said to Peter: 'Go down and depart with them without hesitation, for I have sent them'" (Acts 10, 19). Paul says to the presbyters of Ephesus: "Take heed to yourselves and to the whole flock in which the Holy Spirit has placed you as bishops to rule the Church of God" (Acts 20, 28).

As the Spirit united the community in love, so the same Spirit gave form and structure to the community by an appropriate distribution of functions and offices. The responsible members of the community, as the Spirit's ministers, used the ceremony of "the imposing of hands" to bestow these offices on the persons chosen, and this same imposition of hands passed on to the one appointed a special gift of the Spirit for the right performance of his new task. Thus of the newly chosen first deacons it is written: "These they presented to the apostles, who prayed and laid their hands on them" (Acts 6, 6). Of Paul and Barnabas in the instance quoted above: "Then after fasting and praying they imposed hands on them, and sent them on their way" (Acts 13, 3). Thus Timothy, ruling the Church at Ephesus, is exhorted to "stir up God's grace of office which you have through the laying on of my hands" (2 Tm 1, 6), and "Do not neglect the grace of office you have, which was granted to you by inspired designation with the imposition of the presbyters' hands" (1 Tm 4, 14). And both Timothy and Titus are given long directions for the type of men they should appoint to the offices of bishop and deacon, and are cautioned: "Do not hastily impose hands on anyone" (1 Tm 5, 22).

This community was then ordered and regulated, "Built up on the foundation of the apostles and prophets, with Christ Jesus himself as the chief cornerstone. In him the whole structure is being closely fitted together by the Spirit to become God's temple. In him you too are being fitted by the Spirit into the edifice to become God's dwelling place" (Eph 2, 20-22). John's vision in the Apocalypse of the new city of God, the new Jerusalem, showed too that "The city walls had twelve foundation stones, and on them were the twelve names of the Lamb's twelve apostles" (Ap 21, 14).

Thus those who enter the community are, from the very first chapters of Acts on, "persevering in the teaching of the apostles . . ." (2, 42). And we see the apostles through these early chapters preaching, defending the flock, working miracles in the name of Christ, punishing evildoers in his name.

The apostles establish the new order of deacons in the Church when the need arises (Acts 6). They meet in solemn assembly and resolve the great problem of how the Church should receive the Gentiles: "It has seemed good to the Holy Spirit and to us . . ." (Acts 15, 28).

The evident leader of the apostolic community is St. Peter. He directs the choosing of the successor to Judas (Acts 1), speaks for the community, announcing the good news to the world for the first time on Pentecost (Acts 2), speaks God's judgment on Ananias and Saphira in the name of all the apostles (Acts 5, 2–3). "Peter, with the Eleven" (2, 14), "Peter and the rest of the apostles" (2, 37), "Peter and the apostles" (5, 29) are expressions that appear frequently. Finally, it is to Peter that the decisive revelation is given about taking Gentiles into the Church (Acts 10), and the Council of Jerusalem (Acts 15) gives its decision in accordance with this revelation.

According to the community's own image of itself, it is the remnant of Israel foretold by the prophets, the true Israel, the people God has chosen for himself in Christ. The members' union with Christ through faith and baptism is what makes them God's chosen, for Christ is God's perfect Chosen One, God's true Messiah of Israel. This view provides finally the solution to the problem of how non-Jews can be admitted to the community. For if one now enters the Israel of God by a free act of union with Christ, the Gentiles, under the same divine impulsion as themselves, can enter too. The promises are seen now as directed above all to Christ and available through Christ. He is the Son, he is the Heir, he is in a true sense himself the true Israel, and what the Old Testament foretold of Israel's future has been verified first of all in him, in his death and resurrection. The same fulfillment will come true for all other men to the extent that they accept him and the word of God incorporated in him, and unite themselves to him (Gal 3–4).

This leads finally to the teaching that the community, the Church, is the Body of Christ, not only bearing his image, but united to him as Body to Head, so that the very structure of diverse offices and functions in the Church is comparable to the diversity of parts and functions within one human body. And in all this too, it is the Spirit of Christ who gives life and movement, harmony and order to the whole (Ephesians).

Outwardly there was at first little to distinguish the apostles and their flock from the rest of the Jews. They dressed, looked, acted much like the rest, prayed in the same temple and according to the same ritual, just as they had when Jesus was still with them. The change they had experienced was first of all an internal change; from this a moral reformation followed. It involved adherence to a special group; but outwardly the group was not specially marked.

Gradually, however, differences appeared. First of all, they held their own private gatherings over and above the regular Jewish religious service. For these they would gradually work out their own liturgy. Then certain Jewish rites would gradually strike them as unsuited: could they celebrate, for instance, any other Paschal rite than the one Jesus had left them? Could they use ritual circumcision, promise of the heir to come, without denying Jesus, the heir who was already present? Gradually they came to feel, in one case after another, that they could no longer put their new wine into the same old bottles. Their decision to admit the Gentiles freely intensified all the differences with Judaism. By the time of the pastoral epistles of St. Paul, the break with Judaism seems quite complete.

The very first description of the new Christian community in Acts sets down its very first characteristic point: "They gave steadfast attention to the teaching of the apostles and to union" (Acts 2, 42). The same concern runs through the entire New Testament. We see it in the very latest epistles: "Remember your superiors, since it was they who spoke the word of God to you. . . . Do not be led astray by various strange doctrines. . . . Obey your superiors and be subject to them, since they keep watch over your souls, mindful that they will have to render account" (Heb 13, 7, 9, 17). "If anyone comes to you and does not bring with him this doctrine, do not receive him into your home" (2 Jn 10). "There will be false teachers who will secretly introduce destructive errors" (2 Pt 2, 1). "No prophecy of Scripture is matter for private interpretation" (2 Pt 1, 20).

That is, there is from the first an exact and clearly defined teaching, passed on by the apostles and by the superiors who succeed them in the Church. Paul writes: "I passed on to you as of first importance the message which I also received . . ." (1 Cor 15, 3). And to Timothy: "What you have heard from me in the presence of many witnesses, commend to trustworthy men who will be competent in turn to teach others" (2 Tm, 2, 2). And as to those who depart from the true teaching: "Rebuke them sharply that they may be sound in faith" (Ti 1, 13). "Convince, rebuke, exhort with perfect patience and teaching, for a time will come when they will not endure sound doctrine, but according to their own whims they will multiply for themselves teachers who will tickle their ears. They will turn away from hearing the truth and rather go astray after fables" (2 Tm 4, 2–3).

Against such false teachers, the harshest language is used: "In their greed they will exploit you with glib catchwords. . . . Daring and arrogant . . . like irrational animals they revile what they do not understand. . . . An accursed brood! . . . springs without water, clouds driven by wild wind" (2 Pt 2). "Would that those who are upsetting you would castrate themselves!" (Gal 5, 12.)

Nothing in the New Testament suggests that the beliefs and the practices of the Church were purely or even chiefly a matter of individual inspiration, a movement of simple goodwill where "dogma" held no place. The founding documents of the Christian faith are intolerant of doctrinal deviation, seeing false teaching, heresy, as "the deceiver and the Antichrist" (2 Jn 8), and those who spread it as "these who cause divisions, since they are slaves to their senses, and devoid of the Spirit" (Jude 19). Fidelity to the teaching of the apostles was the key to union, and even the great St. Paul, directly inspired by God, went up to Jerusalem "in consequence of a revelation, and I laid before the Christians there in a general assembly the gospel I habitually preach among the Gentiles, and in private session laid it before those in authority, to make sure that my course of action was not and had not been in vain" (Gal 2, 2).

Noteworthy in the light of our Chapters 6 to 8 is the fact that obedience to the superiors of the Church and faithful adherence to their teaching is presented ordinarily in the context of unity — that is, as we have seen, in a context of real, practical love. Love tends to unity, tends to the forming of a community as a single body; but in practice such unity is impossible and remains only a fiction and a dream unless it means real fidelity to a definitely determined center of unity — and that implies, when the need arises, submission to a definitely determined authority.

Noteworthy too is the fact that not only the Christians as individuals are exhorted to rejoice in a share in Christ's sufferings as their assured route to salvation, but also the individual local churches and the Church in the whole world find their greatest glory and their truest essence in the same. For the Church is the body of Christ, and is to be conformed to him in all things.

Again, just as Jesus died for each one, "for me," so is he said to die for the Church. And when the Apocalypse foretells the long future of the Church, it is a future filled with much tribulation, sorrow, persecution, death — out of all of which the Church constantly rises after the model of Christ to a greater and finally an everlasting glory.

*   *   *

We have seen the external act of baptism by which the believers became members of the community. And we have seen the ritual action of the imposing of hands by which specialized functions and ruling offices in the community were conveyed. Another imposition of hands is mentioned several times in connection with baptism, by which the Spirit was first given to a new Christian (Acts 8, 14–17).

There is another ritual mentioned from the very beginning. It is the special, distinctively Christian gathering, practiced even in the earliest days when the distinctions between the Christian community and the rest of the Jews did not meet the eye. Christians went regularly to the temple to worship. But they also, "met from house to house for the breaking of bread" (Acts 2, 46).

The words might pass unnoticed, were it not for Paul's remark in 1 Corinthians, 10, 16: "The bread which we break, is it not the sharing of the body of Christ? Because the bread is one, we, the many who all partake of that one bread, form one body." He connects it with the "chalice of blessings which we bless" which is "the sharing of blood of Christ," and immediately it is clear that he is referring to the rite he will discuss at length a few verses farther on (11, 23): "The fact is, I have received as coming from the Lord and have passed on to you, how the Lord Jesus on the night of his betrayal took bread into his hands and after he had given thanks, broke it and said: 'This is my body which is given up for you; do this in remembrance of me.' In the same way, after he had finished supper, he took the chalice in his hands and said, 'This chalice is the new covenant sealed with my blood. Do this, as often as you drink it, in remembrance of me.' In reality, every time you eat this bread and drink the chalice of the Lord, you proclaim the Lord's death until he comes" (1 Cor 11, 23–26).

The "breaking of bread" is the "eating of the Lord's supper," the Eucharist. Seeing this connection, we understand remarks like that in Acts 20, 7 that the Christians at Troas "on the first day of the week . . . had met for the breaking of bread." We are dealing with a Christian liturgical rite, the rite solemnly instituted and given to them by our Lord himself the night before he suffered, that they might "eat his flesh and drink his blood" and "have life in them" as John 6 explains.

The apostles had seen the Lord break the bread and tell them it was his body which would be given up. They had seen him pour out the wine and say it was his blood, the blood of a new covenant between God and man, which would be shed for their sakes. The two were present there before the apostles — separately — body to be delivered, blood to be shed. Take the one, he tells them, and eat it. Take this other and drink it. The body, the blood — in the context of his suffering and death.

What he did was a symbolic representation of what was about to happen to him. When you can point here to a man's body

and there to his blood, the man is dead. And that is what he says
— "the body which shall be given, the blood which shall be shed."
The man has undergone a violent death — as Jesus was about to do.

Performing that death symbolically for them, the night before
it happens, he shows that he is going to that death willingly,
consciously, in command and control of himself. That is what
he also makes clear by the words, "offered for you, shed for you."
He goes to death as an act of love for them, because he knows
it will be for their good, indeed is necessary for them "and for
many." "Greater love than this no man has than that he lay down
his life for his friends" (Jn 15, 13). "He loved us and delivered
himself for us" (Eph 5, 2).

This free and willing self-offering, this sacrifice of his, was to
be their sacrifice too. "Do this in memory of me." Do this: come
together in love for one another and for me. Say the words over
the bread, recalling this scene of my deliberate and loving acceptance of the cross. Say these same holy words over your wine,
remembering how I foretold and accepted for your sakes the
shedding of my blood. And you will be admitted to the sharing
of the true body and blood of the Lord (1 Cor 10, 16). "For my
flesh is real food and my blood is real drink" (Jn 6, 55).

They come together to do this in memory of him, and to announce the death of the Lord until he comes. But the memory
of Jesus' sacrifice on the cross, as at the last supper, will remind
them too of their own baptism and the memory of the consecration of themselves to him which they have made. They offer themselves with the bread and wine to be made themselves too into
the body and blood of Christ, to become more and more what he
was and is, to put on his dispositions of loving Sonship in the
face of the hardships and trials which are and will be theirs.
They must eat his flesh and drink his blood if they are to have
life in them. For unless they learn to take up their cross and
follow him they cannot really come after Jesus, have their part
in him, enter with him into the inheritance.

In performing this action in common, they increased their own
unity with one another in Christ Jesus. "One body," Paul calls

them, and "members of the one Lord." And how do they enter into him? By faith, by baptism, and by sharing in the one bread and the one cup of blessing.

Moreover, closer union with Jesus means also an ever more perfect possession by Jesus' Holy Spirit. And this enables them to grow more and more fully into the perfection of love which is the full keeping of the law and the full sinlessness, and ultimately the fullness of the blissful state to which they are called.

Finally, their tendency to love, to sacrifice, to closeness to Christ and devotion to his passion are not left to chance. Salvation is a community affair. And the community regulates these meetings, calls them, sees that they are presided over, and explains the word at them. And as a matter of fact, these gatherings exist only because of the community and inside of the community. The individual actually experiences at them that he is saved in Christ together with his fellow Christians, with and in the real Body of Christ, the Church. Finally, the offering made in these gatherings is always the offering of the Church, before it is that of any or even of all the individuals there present.

CHAPTER 10

Interaction of Imperfect and Perfect

THE sort of interaction and tension which we saw operating between endurance and love should make us cautious about formulating definitive positions which may be the result of too deep an insight into only one part of a complex, subtle, and well-balanced whole. There are many other cases where this kind of dialectic is at work in the New Testament. Often these cases are but different manifestations of a single principle. In the title of this chapter the principle is called the interaction of imperfect and perfect, but that is not the whole story either. It has to do with something particularly hard to attach a name to, because it is unique. It has to do with the touching together of two orders of reality, the point of breakthrough of another world into our own.

Now this other, this supernatural world, is not on the same level of being and action as this world which we spontaneously think of and experience as real. And because it is not on the same level, when it does break through into our world, it does not come in as simply adding something to the reality we know, something which can lie beside, be counted as one more in the same series, with the things we do and see done every day. It is really there when it comes, but not as one more thing. It is there as itself, as a reality on a different level.

For the same reason, when this higher reality breaks into our world, it does not displace the reality which is already here. It does not destroy to make room for itself. It comes from another dimension, and so, even when it arrives, it is present as belonging to another dimension, as continuing still to exist truly on another level.

It comes into our world, and it transforms our world, and it communicates itself to us really and truly — and at the same time it alone for the first time brings us and our world to the perfection proper to us on our own level. We are truly preserved for all we are, with all the perfection and good that is in us on the level of our natural being, precisely because we are granted, over and above our natural being, a taste, share, and experience of a higher being and reality.

The result is that the investigator who approaches phenomena of this God-given life and breakthrough exclusively on the level of this world will indeed find physical and psychological phenomena proper to this our world, operating whole and unimpaired, and even fitting together to make an intelligible story on the level of this world. In the same way, for instance, a chemist, investigating a living thing, according to the methods and with the tools of chemistry, finds in the living thing chemical elements, whole and unimpaired, easily identifiable, and performing their proper functions.

But, to develop this last example somewhat, a biologist investigating the same living thing will, without denying what the chemist has found, find there, with his own methodology and tools, phenomena which are completely characteristic of things that are alive, and which the laws of chemistry do not touch. What does he find over and above the chemicals already listed? Nothing at all that can be added to a list of chemicals. What he finds, and what normally interests him as biologist, are things which seem to make little difference on the chemical level. Yet they are really there. They do not line up with the chemicals, they may not add to the chemical content, they may not destroy any part of the chemical reality in order to make room for themselves. They are on a different level, they belong to a different order of reality and being.

So too our intrusions, our breakthroughs from a higher world. To be seen and appreciated they must be approached with questions, attitudes, methods, proper to their level. Whence are these to come? Unfortunately, we can only approximate them. We can write the history, the psychology, the rational explanations (to some extent) of the recorded events of such breakthroughs. But we, and all mankind with us, sense the presence of another element, not classifiable in our terms, not so easy to point at, and yet clearly there and functioning, making the people who have submitted to it demonstrably different, adding a dimension to their lives and their activity that others do not have; lending them a power which other men feel and recognize at least vaguely as somehow a challenge and a call to themselves to yield themselves to the same force. But when we turn to point at it, to label it, to catalog it, we may not be able to find it. For the blank spaces in human catalogs are shaped to receive events and beings of this world's dimensions. They cannot hold God. Yet when God chooses to reveal himself, he does so. And, catalogable or not, he makes men know that he is really there.

In handling and discussing these points of breakthrough, as theology continually forces us to do, we have to engage in a kind of dialectic. For the imperfect which we know and the perfect we are striving to know and which is really breaking through to us, are both of them present at the same time, and in the same place. The imperfect is transformed because the perfect is also there; in some real way it becomes perfect itself. But it does not become the Perfect.

This is certainly vague, possibly confusing. But the reality we are treating is the most difficult there is to grasp with human minds. We have already touched upon many instances of it in this book, and no doubt our treatments have seemed incomplete, one-sided, and unsatisfactory. We shall therefore take up some of these points again in this chapter. The vagueness, the confusion, the dissatisfaction will not disappear — but they should become easier to face and accept, when we see how, under several different forms, it is the same basic problem which keeps recurring. And at the end of the chapter we shall note that new light is thrown on the Church when we see it as the God-given place in which such breakthroughs regularly happen.

For example, we have seen that the new Christian felt himself marked with the cross of Jesus to such an extent that he found suffering a joy. We have seen that he was transformed in daily life into a new being as it were, and that he really experienced a here-and-now salvation which he could joyfully and confidently preach to the world about him.

We have seen that he lived in perfect love — and that perfect love means perfect sinlessness. "All the believers were one heart and one soul" (Acts 4, 32). "The saints who are at Ephesus" (Eph 1, 1). "All the saints salute you" (Phil 4, 22). "He who is born of God does not sin, but the seed of God remains in him and so he cannot sin" (1 Jn 3, 9).

From these and similar texts it would seem that the original Christians were sinless. Even as late as 200 Tertullian reports the pagans' comment, "See how they love one another." And if there is any accuracy in words, it must be true that in a certain sense they were without sin, they did live in perfect love and charity and generosity, etc. It is in this sense, whatever exactly it is, that the believers of all ages have looked back on that early community of believers with a certain longing, a very real conviction that they had something, some appreciation of what their Christian life was and could be, that later generations have lost.

There is no harm in this. But there is another way of taking those texts and the warm, idealistic pictures of the New Testament that can do much harm. It consists in absolutizing relative statements and failing to balance the one side of the reality by the other. It consists in resting satisfied with a partial picture of the life of the early Church, and, using this as a false norm for the measuring of later ages, arriving of course at sadly deficient conclusions.

Thus results, for example, the puritan cry, "We too must cast out the sinner from our midst" and the rigoristic demand that only the perfect can be members of the Church and counted among those to be saved. Of like mind is the reformer who condemns anything less than the absolute perfection of purity and poverty as a falling away, a corruption of the essence of the

Church of Jesus Christ. Even the orthodox preacher can err in this regard, assailing his hapless flock because they do not shine as stars in the firmament the way the first Christians did. "Where is our charity today? Who would say of this generation of Christians, see how they love one another?"

But from such incomplete and partial views, all shining and holy though they seem, have come many heresies and many schisms, sometimes led by sincere people, who may have seemed among the holiest, best-living Christians of their age. From the long history of the Church, however, it becomes clear what a tragedy this oft-repeated process is. Not only are heresy and schism always evil, dogmatically speaking, but practically and psychologically this particular form of aberration soon demonstrates how unsuited it is to reform mankind. For such sects often enough begin well. But they simply do not endure. Or they endure only at the expense of taking up that precise form of mediocrity and compromise against which they originally rebelled, or worse.

It is so easy to take up the cry of the reformer, the purifier, the simplifier. It is so easy to cry damnation against all those stuffy, mediocre, ordinary people who make up not only the Church but also the business community, the political community, the majority of the social community in which we live — in short, simply the bulk of normal people, the human race, unsatisfactory as it is.

"But," we say, reading the New Testament, "men can be transformed into flames of fire. That is the point of the New Testament message — this change, this transformation, new creation is really possible." Yes — and no. That is the purpose of this chapter. In the earlier chapters we discussed only the "yes" of all this. And a tremendous "yes" it is. The promises of the New Testament along this line — and the historical record of accomplishments — are impressive and real. But they are not the whole story.

There is ample evidence of another side to the picture, evidence drawn direct and without any special pleading from the pages of the New Testament. In Acts, Chapter 4, "the company of those who believed were of one heart and one soul"; but in Chapter 6, "the Hellenists murmured against the Hebrews because their widows were neglected in the daily distribution." In Chapter 4, "no one said that any of the things which he possessed was his own, but they have everything in common." But the first half of Chapter 5 is devoted to the story of Ananias and Saphira who were struck dead for lying to the Holy Spirit, secretly keeping something for themselves.

In Chapter 15, "some men came down from Judea and were teaching the brethren, 'Unless you are circumcised according to the custom of Moses, you cannot be saved.' And Paul and Barnabas had no small dissension and debate with them." And towards the end of Chapter 15, "Barnabas wanted to take with them John called Mark. But Paul thought best not to take with them one who had withdrawn from them in Pamphylia and had not gone with them to the work. And there arose a sharp contention, so that they separated from each other."

And when Peter came to Antioch, Paul "withstood him to his face" (Gal 2, 11). In Paul's letters, one hears of Christians who do not work; of others who have sinned by adultery and incest; there is much discussion of those Christians who are "judaizers," trying to impose on the Gentiles the law of Moses (Acts 21), and they are spoken of in increasingly harsh terms — they want only to glory in your flesh, may they be castrated, etc. (Gal 6, 14; 5, 12). And in Jude and 2 Peter, these same individuals or their successors are causing terrible dissension in the Church and are denounced as sinners of the worst sort. But for all that, they are Christians, baptized, believing — at least they began as such.

In the epistles we find exhortations to avoid almost all the sins there are, and these not simply in general terms as if the New Testament writers were laying down a law to be taught in school, but often in very personal terms of real and warm exhortation — Brethren, don't do this or that — aimed directly at dissuading actual Christians from the practice of certain sins, to which as a matter of fact some of them were showing more than just a passing interior inclination.

It is evident. Christians did fall. Christians did sin. Some of the cases are mentioned for us explicitly — the incestuous man at Corinth, the intemperate at the Lord's supper, those who gave scandal to weaker brethren, some Judaizers, some heretics. Others are mentioned only in general.

What are we to say? At least we must admit that the opinion which pictures the early Christian community as a group of saints, or men perfectly united to one another in the Lord is not the whole picture and hence not the whole truth. We will say that true interpretation of New Testament doctrine must be consistent with the whole New Testament, and take into account all of the evidence therein contained.

We will recur to our principle: judge the Bible by the Bible. We must interpret the teachings of the New Testament according to the practice we see in the New Testament.

But, more deeply still, this problem of sinlessness — which is spoken of both as already possessed and yet to be striven for — is a typical example of the way the contact between two worlds takes place. At first sight it is a matter of reconciling irreconcilable opposites. On more careful examination, it turns out to be a typical theological truth, a picture of the kind of tension that always is present at the point where man meets God.

✿ ✿ ✿

Let us look at some further examples. Not only is man, the Christian, presented as sinless, and yet constantly warring against the reality of sin in his life, but the writings of the New Testament also tell us that we have been saved by Christ dying and rising for us; that we have been saved in baptism; yet that we are and must be working out our salvation in fear and trembling; and that we look forward to our salvation at the day of the appearing of our Lord Jesus Christ.

We learn from the New Testament that the Holy Spirit was given, issuing from the side of Christ, at the moment of his death; that Christ's rising enabled him to pour forth the Spirit upon all men; that Jesus sends forth the Spirit now that he is seated in glory at the right hand of God; that we receive the Spirit when we are baptized, when we receive the laying on of hands; that we live in the Spirit, who dwells in us and pours forth God's love in our hearts.

We are told that Christ's death was our redemption, and that we are expecting our redemption, the resurrection of our bodies. We have been made one with Christ, we have died with him, have been buried with him, have risen and been glorified with him; we were nailed with him to the cross. All this is also the work of baptism. And we are now urged and exhorted to put on Christ; we look forward to growing up in him; and the apostle Paul looks forward to the day when Christ will be formed in us; and at the last day we shall be like our Savior who appears, because we shall see him as he is.

        ❊   ❊   ❊

This introduces the famous question of eschatology, or the question of the end of all things, which has often been the special subject of research in recent years. It is an outstanding example of the perfect/imperfect. The kingdom of God is at hand in the preaching of John the Baptist; it is at hand in the preaching of Jesus; it is present in the midst of us during Christ's lifetime; it is identified with the Church; it is being formed in history; it will be our inheritance in the consummation, when Christ will rule over all.

The end of all things is at hand, is present in the giving of the eschatological gift of the Spirit from Pentecost on, arrives in a fuller sense with the destruction of Jerusalem, comes for each man with his own death and judgment, will be at the last day.

A well-known opinion, widespread among non-Catholic interpreters in the early years of this century, was that Christ's preaching and most of the anomalies of the gospel could be explained in terms of an eschatological message, taking eschatology in the sense of the imminent end of the world. Jesus, according to this theory, preached this imminent end, in a manner not too different from the way that thousands of others since, and probably many a prophet before, had preached the approaching end. His message, and that of the apostles after him, was simply: Be converted, repent, before the final destruction arrives. Only those who believed and were converted and joined the little flock of the end-days could be saved from the terrible destruction about to be wrought. And after the destruction, God would set up his miraculous eschatological kingdom among men in a perfect world for the benefit of the chosen, that is, those who had heard and joined.

Of course, they say, this was a mistake on Jesus' part. But it was a beautiful mistake. He made it the occasion of a preaching about the kind of reform necessary, the purity of life, the whole-hearted devotion to God, the detachment from the things of this world, that had never seen and would never again see its equal on this earth. His mistake has taught mankind many things about the right God-man relationship, and so his teaching has endured. As a matter of fact, his morality and that of the New Testament writers after him is a morality strictly for the end-time, and therefore must be taken with many a grain of salt. But as an expression of a beautiful — though ever unattainable ideal — it remains a challenge and an inspiration to all future ages.

This was, to say the least, a serious oversimplification of a very delicate problem. Those who arrived at it were victims of their own self-limiting methodology. For they operated on the presupposition that the historical events as they had actually occurred had to be dug out from somewhere below the surface of the New Testament account. Those historical events, they took for granted, had to be and would be like historical events as we know them today. We know no incarnate Sons of God. We do know wild-eyed and radical preachers of coming doom. Arrived at such a picture, they then had to interpret the rest of the New Testament in its light. Balances and counterbalances, lights and shadings, were not parts of one picture created ultimately by one Spirit, one Author, but retouches, compromises and adjustments to the reality of a prophecy unfulfilled.

No Catholic could accept such a picture. And today the non-Catholic theologians of the New Testament do not accept it either. Today it is still common to see in most of the preaching and teaching of the New Testament an eschatological reality. But the word "eschatology" has taken on a whole new richness and depth of meaning. It still stands for "the ultimate" — as its Greek root implies. But that ultimate is not necessarily the last moment in time at all. It can be and is last, ultimate, in many different spheres and orders. The term is now used most often to describe precisely that point of juncture between the supernatural and the everyday natural of which we have been speaking. Salvation is eschatological, redemption is eschatological; so is the Spirit, the life of grace and love, the dying and rising with Jesus. But eschatological, far from having to deal with the consummation in fire of this wicked world, has taken on whole new dimensions. "Realized eschatology" some people call it. That wonderful order, that other world, which some Jews and early Christians thought God would call into being after destroying this one, God has (one now sees), according to the teachings of the New Testament, already called into being in Christ. We become part of that new world in our baptism; by deliberate and voluntary struggling, striving, living of the Christian life, we enter into it more and more fully, more and more perfectly according to the measure of — from our part — our deliberate imitation of Jesus and assimilation of ourselves to Christ, and, from God's part, according to his ever more and more perfect bestowing of the Spirit and giving of grace by reason of, in consideration of, the perfect sacrifice of Christ, and of our union with him in it. But that is not a complete explanation either, for "No man comes to me unless the Father draws him" (Jn 6, 44). So that our believing too is not our work but his gift — on the divine level, from God's side. And still, from ours, we continue to act and must act as if everything depended on ourselves; except that we pray for his help, realizing that of ourselves we can do nothing, that all is from him and must always be from him. And so the analysis goes, round and round the one point, which is simply not a point which human words can describe.

*   *   *

This same difficult point with the same problems is at the heart of many of the most difficult discussions of the sacraments too. For in every sacrament, there is to be distinguished the work of the sacrament itself, God's pure gift in grace, and the subjective contribution of him who administers and especially of him who receives the sacrament. Neither can be eliminated from a description which is to be true to the New Testament as a whole. Neither is to swallow up the other. Neither contradicts the fullness of value and truth in the other. The human does not add to the divine, but it is real nonetheless. The divine does not depend on the human but nevertheless always presupposes it in some way or other, and somehow proportions itself to it. These are not contradictions. They are simply the strange phenomena which always occur when two different orders of reality touch. Neglect either aspect at your peril.

Which is more important, which is the really real? Both. The same is true for grace and free will, nature and grace, etc. The same is true of the Church — perfect and made up of sinners, possessing all truth, and progressing painfully from acquisition to acquisition in theological insight, proclaiming the gospel and in constant need of reform.

Paul meant something of the same no doubt when he wrote of his own apostolate: "as deceivers and yet truthful, as unknown yet well known, as ever at death's door, yet, wonder of wonders, we continue to live; as chastised but not killed, as sorrowful yet always rejoicing, as beggars yet enriching many, as having nothing yet possessing everything" (2 Cor 6, 9–10).

The Church is in this point, the juncture of the natural/supernatural, the imperfect/perfect. Perhaps the Church herself is the point. She is in these two worlds at once and at all times. And so she always has two sides, two aspects to her in all things. The one we see all around us and call the Church; the other — the other side of this same Church which we see — is just as real, just as present. But we cannot touch it directly. So every grace she brings us is also simultaneously two-sided; so is every administration of the sacraments. So are our prayers. That is the function, in part at least, of faith — to open up this whole other side of reality to us, so that we can consciously live in it. Still, we live in it at the same time as we live in the first, better-known side of reality; and we use our knowledge of the second, hidden side to govern and guide, stimulate and encourage, our better practice of the controlled, human, psychological, physical side we do possess and see and know.

But finally, the mention of the Church brings us to one last note on this subject. And that is the place of the "institution" in all this: first, in bringing us to these points of juncture of the two worlds and bringing them to us; and, second, in helping us interpret the New Testament as the one complete whole it is.

The New Testament opens to men the most important of these points of contact we have been speaking of. Yet the very nature of such contacts demands a constant tension of already/not yet, perfect/participated, entirely had/to be gained, from God/through us, etc. It follows that some kind of institutionalized organization is the best and probably the only way to keep this New Testament message available to all men through succeeding generations.

Why? Because not all men, not even most, not even a large percentage of them are able to grasp this thing as a whole and fully from the first moment. The ordinary man cannot immediately change his life, reorient his entire being to meet the fullness of the New Testament's demands. Yet his very insight into the message will be conditioned by the extent to which he is already trying to put it into practice. "We ask that you may be filled with a deep knowledge of God's will through perfect spiritual wisdom and insight. Thus your life will be a credit to the Lord and will please him in every respect; you will be fruitful in every kind of good deed, and grow in deep knowledge of God" (Col 1, 9–10).

> . . . since I have heard of the faith in the Lord Jesus which prevails among you, and of the love you have for all the saints, [I] never cease, while giving thanks to God, to remember you in my prayers, that the God of our Lord Jesus Christ, the author of glory, may grant you spiritual wisdom and revelation. May he enlighten the eyes of your mind with a deep knowledge of him, that you may understand of what nature is the hope to which he calls you, what is the wealth of the splendor of his

inheritance among the saints, and what is the surpassing great-
ness of his power toward us believers (Eph 1, 15–18).

True, God makes it possible — if man does his part. Of course,
God also gives man the very wherewithal, the very possibility
of doing his part, and all the help needed in doing it — and again
we go around that same unfathomable point. In short, human
beings are weak, their very faith will not ordinarily be strong
enough to sustain them in the necessary attention to the point
of junction, which they must maintain, "eyes fixed on heaven,"
if the plan of salvation is to work to the fullest. So what is the
solution? Shall only the saints be saved?

No. We shall have an institution, in which the fullness of the
gospel is preached in word and in act so that saints have a chance
to flourish to their fullness, while ordinary people have a chance
to strive, to rise and fall, but rise again — to keep in contact in
spite of themselves with the truth, the light, the grace, the other
world which keeps breaking through to touch them, lift them,
help them. And all this not only at the high moments of their
lives, when their own interior force, cooperation, and faith are
at their strongest and best, but at other moments also, at their
lowest, worse moments when they feel themselves overwhelmed
with sin and selfishness and dirt. The Church will be there —
and through the ministrations of other sinful beings like themselves will be reaching out to them — to take them up again,
cradle them once more as she did from the day of their infant
baptism, and to hold up at last before their dying eyes the
crucifix, and bring them back to God. Those feeble souls who
would indeed like to be good but can't quite manage it — that is
of course the vast majority of us — need and will have the Church.

CHAPTER 11

Behind the Message

THE OLD TESTAMENT

UP UNTIL now we have been looking at the consequences of the message, especially in practical life: What will it mean to hear and believe? What must one therefore do to be saved? Tracing the consequences of the message has led us through the most important Christian virtues, through something of the New Testament notion of the Church, through a little on the sacraments and liturgy. Our analysis could of course continue much farther along the same lines, following the influence of the basic message and the original act of faith into every corner of Christian living, in ever greater detail.

But it is time now to turn our eyes in a different direction. The good news not only led to certain definite results in life and action. The good news also led its hearers to realize certain things were true. The realization followed from their grasp of the good news; but the truths themselves had of course been there all along. They were actually presupposed by the good news.

For example, the Old Testament had announced and foretold God's salvation. Now that the salvation was seen in Christ, one could go back and see what the Old Testament really had meant.

This fact is pointed to again and again in the post-Resurrection accounts in the gospels, as well as in the book of Acts.

Beginning with Moses and going right through the prophets, he interpreted to them whatever is said about himself anywhere in the Scriptures (Lk 24, 27).

"He spoke to us by the way, explaining to us the Scriptures" (Lk 24, 32). "Anything ever written concerning me, whether in the Law of Moses, or in the prophets, or in the Psalms, must needs be fulfilled." He then gave them the key to the understanding of the Scriptures (Lk 24, 44–45).

Peter preaches:

God fulfilled what he had announced through all the prophets: that his Christ should suffer (Acts 3, 18).

At Thessalonica,

. . . as was his custom, Paul went into their meeting and for three Sabbaths reasoned with them from the Scriptures, explaining them and showing that the Christ had to suffer and rise from the dead, and that this is the Christ, "the Jesus whom I proclaim to you" (Acts 17, 2–3).

In defending himself before King Agrippa at Caesarea, Paul states:

Aided to this day by the help of God, I stand here to testify to both high and low, saying nothing beyond what the prophets and Moses said would happen: that the Christ was to suffer, that he, the first to rise from the dead, was to proclaim light to the people and to the Gentiles (Acts 26, 22–23).

To Cornelius Peter says:

To him all the prophets bear witness (Acts 10, 43).

Paul's address in Acts 13 makes it clear that this fulfillment of the prophecies is the fulfillment of God's promises:

"From his [David's] offspring God according to promise brought to Israel a Savior, Jesus. . . . Brothers, children of the race of Abraham, and all among you who fear God, to us the message of this salvation has been sent. Really the citizens of Jerusalem and their leaders fulfilled the words of the prophets which are read every Sabbath by condemning Jesus in their ignorance. Though they found no grounds for the death penalty, they asked Pilate to have him put to death. When they had carried out all that had been written concerning him, he was taken down from the cross and laid in a tomb. But God raised him from the dead, and he was seen during many days by those who had come up with him from Galilee to Jerusalem. So they became witnesses of him to the people.

"We now bring you the Good News that God has fulfilled the promises made to our forefathers for us, their children, by raising Jesus, as also it is written in the second Psalm, 'You are my son; this day have I begotten you.' And to show that he has raised him from the dead, never again to return to decay, he has thus said,

> 'I will give fulfillment of the holy
>   and unfailing promises made to David.'

For this reason in another Psalm he says, 'You will not let your Holy One see decay.' "Now after he had served God's purposes for the benefit of his own generation, David fell asleep and was gathered to his fathers, and did see decay. But he whom God raised to life did not see decay. Be it known to you, therefore, brothers, that it is by him that forgiveness of sins is proclaimed to you and through this one everybody who believes is acquitted of all the sins of which you could not be acquitted by the Law of Moses. Beware, therefore, that what is said in the prophets may not prove true of you,

> 'See, you despisers, then wonder, and perish,
>   because I do a deed in your days,
> A deed which you will not believe,
>   if anyone relates it to you' "

(Acts 13, 23–41).

We said in Chapter 2 that the apostles saw the promises turned inside out. This reversal of viewpoint is summed up in: "this, . . . is the gist of the Scriptures: the Messias must suffer and on the third day rise from the dead. Furthermore: in his name the need of a change of heart and forgiveness of sins must be preached to all the nations" (Lk 24, 46–47). This is the key point and the transforming point. Israel had been looking forward to the fulfillment of the promises especially in and through the coming of her great anointed one and the new age which he would usher in. Jesus had claimed to be that anointed one, and they had believed it. Then he had apparently failed, been rejected by the people whom he should have been saving. It seemed then that he was not God's chosen after all. Then God had raised him up from the dead and made it evident that Jesus *was* the Christ.

But if so, then the promises had been, were being, and would be fulfilled in him after all — in him who suffered and died! Then one is forced to go back and rethink what happened to him in the light of the promises. And one must reread and rethink the promises in the light of what happened to him.

And what is the result? The result is that they find that which they begin to preach: that the Christ, God's chosen, had suffered according to God's plan — that part of the idea of salvation was the enduring of suffering and death. They find that Christ's moment of suffering and death, his moment of greatest trial and failure, was the moment of his greatest triumph. They find that the most unjust act, the most repellently unjust climax to a faithful and good life — as Christ has experienced it — was in reality, and in God's plan, only the preparation of the greatest glory. It was necessary that he should suffer — and so enter into his glory. For resurrection presupposes death. Jesus then laid down his life "in order to take it up again," (Jn 10, 17).

But what does this suddenly mean for this people of Israel after so long a series of promises unfulfilled, always to be looked for, a salvation always in the future or in the past, but never apparently actually present? Looking back, they see how the promises had always been given in difficult moments, had demanded faith in God's working the apparently impossible. Abraham was to have abundant posterity, enough to make him a proverb of blessing among the nations — but at the age of one hundred years, with a wife over ninety, the son through whom that great progeny was to come had not yet been born.

He was to inherit the whole land of Canaan, but, as Stephen's discourse in Acts points out, "He had hardly set foot in it as yet." Moses was to save the people out of bondage, but they did not understand "that through him God was giving them deliverance." Him "they disowned . . . were unwilling to obey, thrust aside." The people were to enter the promised land, but had to keep faith and keep hoping for forty years in the wilderness. And as to the posterity of David, the throne of Israel — some of the greatest praise of it, and some of the greatest promises concerning it had been put into the Bible at the time when the kingdom was actually at its weakest, least powerful, least promising, least magnificent. The future might of Israel had been announced as an object of belief in the course of the captivities and enslavements. And as a matter of fact, that is the way the Jews had believed in it. They hoped against hope. No word shall be impossible with God. And as, down through the centuries, God had granted them from time to time partial fulfillments of what they hoped for — for they had inherited the land, though it did not flow with milk and honey; they had been delivered from exile after seventy years; they had been saved from the oppressing Antiochus, etc. — each time that they had received partial fulfillments of what was promised, they knew it had been only when they had turned to God in prayer, confessed their sins and unfaithfulness, and then, even while bearing the trial as justly deserved, had never ceased to hope.

If Jesus was the Christ — and, since God had raised him from the dead, he obviously was — then it followed that what had happened to him had happened according to a divine plan. It was therefore no simple coincidence when they saw that the same elements occurred in what had happened to him as had been occurring in the salvation history of the people of Israel. He was the greatest example of the good and just servant of God, and he received from God the hardest of fates. He bore what happened to him without losing confidence in God, without cursing his enemies. He suffered not for his own wickedness but, as he had himself proclaimed in advance, for the sins of others, of the many. And in all this he had won the most high favor with God, as was shown in God's raising him from the dead.

But if he was the Christ and if this was God's way of salvation, then this clarified their whole history. They had experienced trial enough. And in the early days when the people had often wandered from God to other gods, to idols, to open sin, it had not been too hard to understand what was happening when God inflicted some trial on them. He was warning them. He was punishing them, he was calling them back to himself.

But in the days after the exile, after the reform of Ezra, they had really been trying to live up to the divine will, really been trying to keep God's law, studying it day and night, and really trying to make it the rule, the be-all and end-all of their existence. And still they had been afflicted, still they were conquered, disgraced, bounced about from one master to another. Still there was no sign at all of the great restoration and triumph they expected. Why not? What were they doing wrong?

Now, if they believed in Jesus as the Christ, they knew that nothing was necessarily wrong. This was God's pattern of salvation. A just and holy Israel could well be suffering, and suffering because of sin. But the sins were not necessarily her own. The world, the whole world, was living according to a pattern of evil, selfishness, cruelty, lust. The life of the just in such a world was a life of being persecuted, taken advantage of, being exploited, mocked, made to suffer, killed. This they had experienced. This they knew. This was not good news, nor indeed was it news at all. But, if Christ was their Christ, if Jesus crucified was their salvation, they suddenly saw another pattern being imposed upon, indeed emerging from, the old pattern of sin, suffering, and death.

For in Christ's defeat had been his greatest triumph. His dying had been the cause of his coming to life in glory. His suffering had been his own final vindication, and the very judgment on his accusers and murderers. Now in Christ, they could see what God had been saying to them all along: that all good things do come to the man who gives himself wholly and unreservedly to God no matter how trying the circumstances. They could see that the worst possible fate which could unjustly befall a man can be always turned into triumph. It is an insight into the secret of the cross, "the foolishness of the cross" of which St. Paul writes. God's chosen must suffer, but, remaining faithful, he triumphs over suffering and death itself. Jesus did this, embodying in himself all of Israel. And Israel had been and now was being called to go on doing this too.

Here the old pattern was broken. The old pattern, learned from the original covenant of God with Israel, had been this: sin was followed by punishment; punishment caused the people to turn away from sin and back to God; if they purified their lives completely, observed his law perfectly, they would be saved out of their punishment and be blessed.

The new pattern, beginning with the new covenant in Christ was this: if the people (or the individual) found themselves in misery, they knew it came from sin. But they had to face the fact that no matter how hard they tried, they would never be able to purify themselves from sin completely, never of themselves keep God's law perfectly. Rather, believing in Jesus crucified as God's redemption, they voluntarily associated themselves with his perfect act of submission to God and love of God and patience in suffering, voluntarily agreed to go on bearing the suffering which was a part of their living the good life and necessary to it, as an expiation for their own sins and for the sins of others. Not that they were capable of promising and performing these exalted virtues any more easily than the rest of God's law. Not of themselves. But they had Christ crucified "vividly portrayed before their eyes" (Gal 3, 1) and they could look to him, point to him, reach out to him. This was the mark and seal they accepted to be set upon their own lives. Here was the perfect human offering to God, the perfect human disposition before God, and in will, in intention, in hope, they made it their own. They prayed that God be more pleased with the merits of that one perfect act of Christ than he was displeased with all their own sins, and that, looking to the merits of that act rather than to their own faults, he would grant them life with Christ.

Doing this, they found the deliverance they wanted granted them. They experienced the gift of the Holy Spirit, the forgiveness of past sins in union with Jesus; they experienced a new power to avoid sinning in the future; they found, if not relief from suffering, something better — the ability to bear suffering with joy; and they received the assurance of a complete relief from all evil which would soon arrive, when they too with Christ would rise from the dead to possess the kingdom now inaugurated in him.

Here too is the solution to the problem that had been intriguing them in recent centuries, appearing in the later, the so-called Wisdom literature of the Bible, and especially in the book of Job. How could the just man suffer? The answer was given partly already in the Old Testament books. But the answer never had been, never could be given with such force, such clarity, and such compelling power, making belief and practice possible for all times, as it was here in this one superinstance: the greatest injustice to the most holy and just Person who had ever lived, the Son of God himself. His complete acceptance, out of obedience and love, worked the greatest conceivable human triumph.

Moreover, in this very act had been fulfilled the greatest of the promises, the long-hoped-for beginning of the resurrection of the dead. To this St. Paul referred when he said: "Now because of the hope in the promise made by God to our fathers I stand here on trial. This promise our twelve tribes hope to attain as they serve God earnestly day and night. It is about this hope, O king, that I am accused by the Jews. Why is it deemed incredible that God should raise the dead?" (Acts 26, 6–8.)

This is also what St. Paul meant when he wrote: "He is the beginning, the first to rise from the dead . . . " (Col. 1, 18) and that he preached: "I stand here to testify to both high and low, saying nothing beyond what the prophets and Moses said would happen: that the Christ was to suffer, that he, the first to rise from the dead, was to proclaim light to the people and to the Gentiles" (Acts 26, 22–23). And he wrote to the Corinthians: "Christ has truly been raised from the dead, the first fruits of those that have fallen asleep in death" (1 Cor 15, 20), continuing: "Christ the first-fruits, then Christ's own, when he comes."

So, in summary, where was the good news and the fulfillment of promises? First of all, God raises the dead. Second, God's plan of salvation is consummated in Christ. Third, he who takes God's plan of salvation as his own, believing in Jesus, the crucified failure, as God's anointed, as God's salvation, as the hope of the world, experiences a share in that salvation, in that glory and life, which the apostles had seen and could bear witness to in the risen Jesus, and which they received themselves in the Spirit. Fourth, the rest of the divine promises were about to be fulfilled, through and in the risen Jesus. A new kingdom of peace and happiness was coming into being for all those who accepted the offered way of salvation and made the decision to live according to the pattern of Christ in his new community, the new Israel, the true Remnant, the Church. Moreover, the great miraculous consummation itself was caught glimpse of in the risen Jesus. Besides, Jesus had foretold it — and his announcements were now proved true, confirmed, in his rising. And above all he himself was the first step in the final consummation, and in him it was actually made visible before men's eyes.

This was the basically changed viewpoint on the Old Testament. Once grasped, it was seen to give a new slant to almost everything in the Bible. For the Old Testament as the New was a message of salvation, was good news, gospel. It was even "the very same gospel," as St. Thomas Aquinas explains in his commentary on the opening verses of Galatians. It too called for faith, for believing as true what God spoke in his promises, for firm and loyal adhesion to the one true God. One who searched carefully and pondered the whole history of the people, its successive good fortune and bad, turning to God and away from him, could make out the salvation pattern which is death and resurrection for him who believes and loves and perseveres. The same pattern could be picked out in the structure of the writings of the prophets.

God does not change. And it was the same loving God who was revealing himself in the Old Testament as in the New. The God of the law and the prophets who had called, pleaded, and cajoled through the long history of the people, speaking to them in diverse ways through the prophets, calling to the people to turn to the Lord their God, now finally sent his only Son, now spoke to them through and in this Son, and was in Christ reconciling the world to Himself, when Christ finally, being lifted up from the earth, began to draw all things to himself.

St. Paul's attacks on the Judaizers and rejection of circumcision and the law for Gentile converts stems from the insight that once one had received God in this new way, this direct manner, it was just nonsense, it was falsehood, to want to return to the old way — it was, says St. Thomas, to imply that the Old Testament had preached another and different gospel, to imply that faith and love, baptism and incorporation into Christ and his Church were not sufficient; it was to give up the perfect expression of God's salvation and God's covenant with men to return to the imperfect foreshadowing. For that reason Paul had to reject and attack this tendency.

But the same St. Paul who could lash out in anger at the Judaizers could still say of the Jews: "Theirs is the adoption as sons, theirs the glory, the covenants, the legislation, the worship, and the promises. The patriarchs are theirs, and from them has been derived the human nature of Christ" (Rom 9, 4–5). He could warn the Romans that Gentiles have salvation only insofar as they are grafted into the tree which is Israel, a tree whose roots are Abraham, Isaac, and Jacob, a tree of which the natural-born Jews are more fitting members than anyone else. He could write that "God has not rejected his people," and that he himself would do anything possible for their salvation — even to the extent, if necessary, of being himself cut off from Christ — so much at heart did he have their concerns and interests and love.

The New Testament writers in general, once they had been given to see the unity of God's plan and the fulfillment of the old salvation scheme in Christ, could and did go on to apply to Christ all of the specific concrete details of the Old Testament salvation as well. They could and did refer to Christ all the texts which promised future salvation: texts that referred to persons who were God's instrument of deliverance, like Zorobabel, Hezekiah, even Cyrus the Great; texts that referred to material things, like the tabernacle, the temple, the ark of the covenant, the written law itself; texts that referred to the people as a whole. Whenever the Bible spoke of true salvation, of the true servant of God, of union with God and God dwelling in the midst of his people, of men reaching up to God by faith and love and sacrifice, they could see now — in the light of their general new insight — that those things were only imperfectly verified in the examples explicitly mentioned in the Old Testament, but that they were perfectly verified for the first time in Jesus Christ.

This same insight with these consequences was the beginning of a long history of typological and even allegorical interpretation of the Old Testament in patristic and later theology down to our own day. Modern scripture research has strengthened the foundations of this type of interpretation as it has found out more and more accurately how much of type and symbolism and prophecy was formally intended by the Old Testament authors themselves when they wrote many of these things.

CATHOLIC DOGMA

Behind the kerygma lay the whole Old Testament, the word as it had been taught and preached in Israel for centuries. The New Testament message can never be separated from this foundation and preparation in understanding any more than it was ever separate in reality.

But we can and must now go behind the kerygma in another sense too if we are to get something of the picture of the whole New Testament. For the good news not only gave a new understanding of the ancient scriptures. It also presupposed and implied many specific truths about the real world. If Jesus' death and resurrection are truly our salvation, what must Jesus himself be? Who must he be? What must God be like to have given us such a salvation as we have experienced? What is our present state in regard to God? How did we get into it? How does Jesus' activity touch us, reach us, have its effect in us?

This material, the answers to these and similar questions, is what we today most spontaneously think of as theological, dogmatic material: the nature of God, One and Three; the creation, elevation, and fall of man; the Incarnate Word and the redemption he wrought; grace; the last things. These things are the heart of an ordinary course of Catholic theology.

These truths, certain definite answers to definite questions, must lie behind the kerygma if it is to make any real sense. Believe the good news of salvation in Christ and you implicitly believe that certain set of answers.

It is difficult for us today to determine exactly how explicitly conscious of the right and exact answer on each of these points the very earliest Christians were. For they did not write dogmatic treatises aimed at expounding these background truths. What they wrote about and proclaimed was the good news. They referred to these truths which were presupposed in the good news, when it was necessary to refer to them in order to straighten out some misinterpretation in practice or teaching, or, most frequently, to make stronger and more effective their exhortation to the living out of the good news.

Nevertheless, a definite set of dogmatic truths was from the first implied in and presupposed by the good news. This is an objective fact, not dependent at all on whether or not the preachers always adverted to the fact. For instance, we saw earlier something of how hesitant the apostles were at first about going to preach to the Gentiles, and of how uncertain they were whether the non-Jews should be obliged by the external cere- monial, dietary, and other observances of the Old Law. For a long time they were not sure of the answers, they disputed about them among themselves. And yet, when a final decision had to be given, there was only one decision possible; for, whether they had noticed it before or not, the answer to their doubts was built right into the message which they preached. If Christ dying and rising is our salvation, a salvation which comes to us substantially in faith and baptism, then the question on Jewish observances and on the universal availability of this salvation is settled al- ready, right there in the heart of the kerygma. And they, whose preaching and teaching was guided by the indwelling Spirit, and whose whole lives were formed around the effort to actualize that good news, to put flesh on it, to grow up in Christ, could not adopt a definitive solution to these individual questions which would be out of accord with everything else they believed and felt and lived. So it was with the other principal truths.

We want to pick out a few of the more important of these

truths which the New Testament shows were already at that time clearly seen and taught as connected with the good news. We will not be able to make anything like a thorough study here. To do so would be eventually to cover the whole territory of dogmatic theology. Besides, much of this material is available already in standard New Testament introductions and in the introductions to individual New Testament authors: short summaries of what each one taught and wrote regarding the great mysteries of Christianity. Histories of dogma also regularly gather together the texts which prove that later definitions of the Church were well grounded in New Testament doctrine. We shall content ourselves here with a brief sketch of a few points, stressing above all their intrinsic connection with the kerygma.

❂   ❂   ❂

There are two ways of getting at these truths. The first is an extension of what we have seen in the first part of this chapter: approaching what Christ has done for us through the language and thought patterns of the Old Testament.

For example, Paul says: "Christ loved us and delivered himself for us as an offering to God, a sacrifice that has an agreeable fragrance" (Eph 5, 2). In itself, this was a natural way for someone of Paul's background to speak of a great and generous act of love which someone had performed at great difficulty to himself. Thus when Paul receives a generous gift from the Christians of Philippi, he says, "I am fully supplied now that I have received from Epaphroditus what you sent. It was a sweet aroma, a sacrifice acceptable and well pleasing to God" (Phil 4, 18). And of his own apostolic labors and approaching death, he writes: "I am already being poured out in sacrifice" (2 Tm 4, 6).

But the epistle to the Hebrews takes the same idea of sacrifice, and, comparing Christ's act of love and self-giving with all the material, animal sacrifices of the Old Testament, shows how men can come fully to true union with God, forgiveness of sin, the heights of divine favor and blessing, through the sacrifice of Christ. Those former things were a figure, a shadow; the reality is the perfect act of obedience and love of the perfect Man. "You took

no pleasure in burnt offerings and sin offerings. Then I said:
'Here I am; I have come to do your will, O God'" (Heb 10, 6).

And so throughout the New Testament, Christ's self-offering
for us, for our sins, to bring us to God, to unite us to God, reconcile us to God, turn us to God, is described in terms of the Old
Testament with the obvious point that here is the final fulfillment,
the perfection of what God gave imperfectly then. Thus, for example, Christ's death is a redemption, a liberation, a salvation,
as the Old Testament had used those same terms for God's leading the people out of Egypt and taking them to himself and for
his bringing the people back from exile in Babylon. Christ's
death is a circumcision, a slaying of the Paschal lamb, a drinking
of God's chalice, a triumphing over the powers of hell and of
this earth. All these are applications to Christ of the great things
God had done and of the language the prophets had used in the
Old Testament to describe God's glorious works for the sake of
Israel or Israel's special union with God.

❋ ❋ ❋

But there is a second aspect, another way of coming to the
truths which lie behind the message. For instance, the message
says that God has sent his salvation in Jesus Christ; that Jesus,
exalted as the Lord to the right hand of God, sends forth from
there the Holy Spirit upon the believers. Unless there exist
Father, Son, and Holy Spirit, this message does not make
much sense.

No one but God bears the name of the Lord, no one but God
sends forth the Spirit of God. This was fundamental catechism
for the Jews. But Jesus did both these things. Yet Jesus, though
he had spoken of himself as one with the Father, though he
had manifested the divine in all he said and did, though he had
claimed and exercised divine prerogatives, demanding for himself
the place which was God's place at the center of religious thought,
faith, and religious activity — still, Jesus had always spoken of
God, his Father, as of Another, as of Someone Else. Jesus was
not the Father. The Father was the God of the Old Testament.

Still, there was only one God. Jesus taught it as had the

prophets, and, when asked for the greatest commandment in the Law, Jesus cited the *Hear O Israel*, that prayer which above all others stresses the divine unity: "Hear O Israel, the Lord our God is one Lord. And you shall love the Lord your God with all your heart and with all your soul and with all your strength . . . " (Deut 6, 4–5).

Again, the Spirit does the works of God. The Spirit forms men to the divine image in Christ. The Spirit pours forth God's love in their hearts. The Spirit changes the face of the earth. He is of the divine order. Yet they experience him as a Person who speaks to them and directs them. And still there is only one God.

Such arguments are not elaborated in the New Testament. But the facts are stated. The facts are a part of explaining the good news. But the facts cannot be fitted together to make sense unless behind those facts lies the Catholic dogma of the one God and the three divine Persons.

The New Testament writings do not stop to elaborate a treatise on the Trinity. Even the simple statement that there are three Persons in God does not even once occur. And yet the New Testament is constantly showing the three Persons at work in the world, in us, and it outlines over and over again our approach through Christ in the Spirit to the Father. Questions about the exact relations of these three to one another have not yet been posed. But later when the questions do arise, the answers are already predetermined by the shape of the kerygma.

Thus Nicea defined that Christ was true God of true God, consubstantial with the Father. The first Council of Constantinople defined that the Spirit was true God, equally to be adored with the Father and the Son. Both councils appeal to the perpetual tradition of the Catholic Church. Some historians say the evidence for such perpetual tradition is very broken: several of the early Christian writers say nothing of it, some use completely other terms and deny the fitness of the ones defined, some seem to speak of only two Persons, etc. Where was the tradition in their time? Either, they say, it had been forgotten, or it never existed; unless it was being passed on in secret somewhere in the Church.

But in fact the tradition was present from the first and was passed on unchanged, up to the time of the definitions. Where? In the teaching and preaching and living of the message that Christ was our salvation. Without the three Persons in the one God, the kerygma made no sense. But the kerygma did make sense: Christ was our salvation. Without consubstantiality, and distinction of persons and nature, "three Persons in one God" would be meaningless. But it was not meaningless, for we were saved in Christ.

The words, even the exact concepts, could not be present until the questions about them arose. But the truth itself was there, firmly fixed and determined, in the message.

The same was true of the Incarnation. Did the earliest Christians hold that Jesus was the preexistent Son of God? As far as the earliest preaching goes, it is hard to see that they stopped to ask themselves this question. They had known him first as a man; a prophet, a mysterious and wonderful man to be sure, but still a man. Now something magnificent had happened to him, he had shown depths of reality, treasures of wisdom and knowledge, of which they perhaps had never even dreamed. But still it could have been some time before they asked themselves, What was he before we came to know him?

They used divine titles for him, making him equal to God. And of course they knew that no one "becomes" God. When they asked themselves the direct question, only one answer was possible. The answer was implied as fixed and determined in what they had to preach — Christ crucified; "to the Jews certainly a stumbling block and to the Gentiles absurdity, but to those who are called, to the Jews and Greeks alike, Christ the power of God and the wisdom of God" (1 Cor 1, 24).

The same is true of all which will become the later theology on grace. Salvation is given in Christ, the crucified and risen. It is there to be taken by all who believe. But it is there completely as God's gift. "God himself will come to save us."

So marked, indeed, has been God's love for the world that he gave his only-begotten Son: everyone who believes in him is not to perish, but to have eternal life (Jn 3, 16).

> . . . sanctification brought about by God through faith in
> Jesus Christ. It comes to all believers, as there is no discrimina-
> tion. All have sinned and lack the approval of God. They are
> sanctified freely by his grace through the redemption which is
> in Christ Jesus (Rom 3, 22–24).

And even the ability to make the act of faith itself is God's gift:
"Nobody is able to come to me unless the Father . . . draw him"
(Jn 6, 44). Where, then, is there any reason for boasting? It is
excluded (Rom 3, 27).

The picture of man without grace is "by nature" a child "of
wrath," "without God in this world," and is finally summed up in
Paul's great comparison of Christ and Adam as two heads of the
human race, one by his disobedience the father of sin and death,
the other by obedience the source of grace and life.

o   o   o

This is, all in all, only a partial, sketchy listing. But it is perhaps
enough to show how the points which were to occupy much of
later theology were already given as implied in the preaching
of the one central fact. Not that they had to go through a process
of deductive reasoning to arrive at all these points. Many they
knew already from the Old Testament. These they saw now in a
new light, as leading up to the salvific death and resurrection of
Jesus the Christ. Others, which they had learned only from Jesus
or from the revelation of the Spirit, they saw as directly connected
with the same core announcement. Their salvation in the cross and
resurrection came because the man who died was God himself
come to save them; it consisted in the fact that the very Spirit of
God was poured out upon them, that God who was somehow three
as well as one, abided with them and in them.

It is the message and its practical consequences which are in
the forefront of their consciousness. That is why finally when
they have to speak out against heresy, they attack it first of all
because it corrupts the message and eventually makes impossible
the new life in Christ.

As there were false prophets among the people of Israel, so among you there will be false teachers, who will secretly introduce destructive errors. These teachers will go so far as to deny even the Master who redeemed them. In this way they will bring down on themselves swift destruction. Many will follow them in their acts of debauchery (2 Pt 2, 1–3).

Avoid profane and empty babblings, for those who engage in such talk will contribute much to impiety and their doctrine will spread like gangrene. Of this sort are Hymenaeus and Philetus, who have wandered from the truth by saying that the resurrection has already taken place. They are destroying the faith of some (2 Tm 2, 16–18).

If anyone teaches otherwise and does not agree with the sound instruction of our Lord Jesus Christ and that doctrine which makes for piety, he is swollen with pride. . . . These give rise to envy, quarreling, slander, base suspicions, wrangling among men whose minds are corrupt and deprived of truth, and who believe that religion is a source of gain (1 Tm 6, 3–5).

Beloved, do not believe every spiritual manifestation, but test them to see whether they are of divine origin, because many, equipped with counterfeit gifts, have gone forth into the world. You can recognize such manifestations as of divine origin by this test: Every manifestation that acknowledges Jesus Christ incarnate is of divine origin. No manifestation that denies Jesus is of divine origin. On the contrary it is a manifestation that originates with the Antichrist. You have heard he is on the way. Well, at this moment he is already in the world (1 Jn 4, 1–3).

Let us love one another. . . . I beg this of you, because many deceivers have gone forth into the world, men who do not acknowledge the coming of Jesus Christ in the flesh. Here you have the deceiver and the Antichrist. Look to yourselves, so that you do not lose what we have gained, but that you may receive a full reward. Anyone who forges ahead of Christ's doctrine and fails to remain true to it, does not hold on to God. He who remains true to this doctrine holds on to both the Father and the Son. If anyone comes to you and does not bring with him this doctrine, do not receive him into your home. Do not even speak words of greeting to him, for he who does so shares in his wicked deeds (2 Jn 5–11).

THE WORD IN THE WORD INCARNATE

CHAPTER 12

Toward Unity

TO BREAK down into distinct propositions and argue out in some logical detail the message of our redemption in Christ, the core of our whole faith and our whole religious life, is a long, slow process. We must not forget as we engage, or attempt to engage, in such an analysis, that the message was not presented originally on that level or in that form. Such analysis and explanation is rather the work of theology. It comes later. The God-given true religion, which is for all men, had to present that message in a way which could strike home to the hearts of all men. That is why the message first of all *happened* — was something that came in the flesh, in an individual, a man, whose love men could see and feel, whose example could stir just as deeply and truly all those men who could never even begin such an analysis as well as those who would in later centuries find in that same reality unending food for thought and unlimited abysses of truth about God and man, reality and life.

So as not to lose our perspective in the course of this study, it may be well here to recall briefly some of the more concrete, summary forms in which this message and implicitly the whole of Catholic truth was presented in that first age. Capsule accounts of the kerygma itself we have already seen in abundance. And the Eucharist, as we have seen, is also the gospel in miniature. But there were others. Already in that first century, to judge by the indications and relics archaeology has found for us, a physical, plastic summary of the teaching came into use, the same one which even today is the most common and widespread of all — the cross.

Crosses have been found on first-century sarcophagi in Palestine. A cross was found on the wall of a small upper chamber of a house in Herculaneum, certainly dating from before the year 70. Moreover literary sources in the following, the second century, already speak of the practice of marking the cross on one's body in a symbolic gesture which meant "Christian." And they speak of it as of a practice already venerable with age.

Does this mean they neglected the resurrection? Hardly. St. Paul says often that he preaches "the scandal of the cross," "Christ crucified," "the cross of Christ," etc., and yet if ever man preached the resurrection it was certainly he. No, it is rather that the cross is such an apt and easy physical symbol — easy to make, easy to recognize, and an easy and quick means for the instructed Christian to recall the whole of the message in one single, simple meaningful gesture or sign. There is moreover the fact that the very anomaly of exalting the cross, of placing in the public view with pride, esteem, and affection, that which was in itself a mark of shame, punishment, and disgrace — like a hangman's rope or an electric chair — that very anomaly proclaims and makes clear that this cross is not just a cross, but means suffering transformed into glory and joy, death into life, failure into triumph.

We unite the cross sign today with the Trinitarian formula, In the name of the Father and of the Son and of the Holy Ghost. Did the first generation of Christians do this? They could have. The Trinitarian formula existed, and existed in a central position — "Go, therefore, and make all nations your disciples; baptize them in the name of the Father and of the Son and of the Holy Spirit" (Mt 28, 19). Such a union of the formula with the cross as we have it in the sign of the cross today gives us a most excellent gospel in miniature, a tiny but perfect summary of the Christian message, experience, and life. In the name of God, the God known, preached, and loved from the entire Bible, God who has providentially and lovingly arranged all things for our good, we accept the cross which he has sent us as Christ accepted his, and we do so in the name of Christ Jesus, God's Son, who, dying on the cross, worked out our salvation. This salvation, with our acceptance of the cross in submission and love, comes to us in the Holy Spirit, who is given to us. This is the Spirit of Jesus, who keeps us one with Jesus in a perpetual attitude of sacrifice and love, and who abides with us as pledge of our eternal life to come with this our Triune God.

Whether Christians began already in the first generation making the sign of the cross on themselves together with the invocation of Father, Son, and Holy Spirit, we cannot be sure. Still if the cross is taken as standing for what Jesus did for us, and the Trinitarian formula is taken as a summing up of the great sweep of the divine plan, from before all ages down to the end of ages, then the two elements have a natural affinity for each other and clamor to be united. We do find them united from very early times — late first and early second century at least — in another gospel in miniature: in the earliest Christian creeds.

The basic structure of a creed is the same one we have today in the Apostles' Creed and in the Nicene Creed which we recite at mass. And this same pattern has been basic to all the official creeds of the Church through the centuries. Different general councils modify one aspect or another of a previous creed, enlarge upon a disputed point of the time in order to clarify it, but the basic structure, pattern, and outline is the same. It is the structure, pattern, and outline of our salvation: the kerygma, the truth about Jesus, set in the eternal divine plan which follows the procession of the divine Persons, Father, Son, and Holy Spirit.

A creed opens with the Father: "I believe in God the Father almighty, Creator of heaven and earth"; goes on to the Son: "and in Jesus Christ his only Son, our Lord." This is expanded into the main points of the message about Jesus: "who was conceived of the Holy Spirit, born of the Virgin Mary, suffered under Pontius Pilate, was crucified, died, and was buried. He descended into hell. The third day he rose again from the dead. He ascended into heaven, sitteth at the right hand of God the Father almighty. From thence he shall come to judge the living and the dead."

These points give Jesus' origin as true Son of God, and then move immediately into his suffering, death, burial, descent and resurrection, glorification and future return: the same message about Jesus which the gospels and the preaching conveyed.

"I believe in the Holy Spirit: the holy Catholic Church, the communion of saints, the forgiveness of sin, the resurrection of the body, and life everlasting." The third part of the creed is built around the Holy Spirit, the third Person of the Blessed Trinity. In him salvation comes to each of us through the Catholic Church, a salvation which consists in the shared life of all sanctified in him, and in the forgiveness of sin, and which looks forward to full salvation of the resurrection of the body and eternal life with God. All these are the works of the Spirit, just as the works of the Creator God known from the Old Testament and later identified as Father of our Lord Jesus Christ are described in the first part of the creed, and just as the passion, death, and resurrection of the incarnate second Person are described in the central portion.

The Nicene Creed, to look briefly at another example, leaves practically unchanged the first section, but adds to the second a much more careful and explicit identification of the second Person who became man: "And in one Lord Jesus Christ, only-begotten Son of God, born of the Father before all ages; God of God, Light of Light, true God of true God; begotten not made, of one substance with the Father, through whom all things are made. Who for us men and for our salvation came down from heaven, and was made flesh of the Holy Spirit from the Virgin Mary — and became a man. Crucified too for us, under Pontius Pilate, he suffered and he was buried. And he arose on the third day according to the Scriptures, and he ascended into heaven, sits at the right hand of God the Father almighty; from there he will come to judge the living and the dead; and of his kingdom there will be no end."

Besides the more precise description of the person of Jesus (the question being especially argued at the time the creed was prepared was his exact relation to God the Father and Creator), this second part of the creed makes the kerygma itself more explicit than does the Apostles' Creed. "For us men" the Son becomes man. "For us" he suffers and dies. He rises from the dead "according to the Scriptures."

The third part of the creed, concentrating on the Holy Spirit, makes his works too more explicit, his role in the full redemption, and especially too — after the debates of the first Council of Constantinople — his relation of equality as true God with the Father and the Son. "And in the Holy Spirit, Lord and Vivifier, who proceeds from the Father and the Son; who with the Father and the Son is at the same time, in the same way, adored and with them glorified; who has spoken through the prophets. And in one holy Catholic and apostolic Church. I confess one baptism for the remission of sins. And I look forward to the resurrection of the dead, and the life of the age to come."

Such a creed already contains considerable elaboration. Three centuries of theological speculation and Christian experience had preceded it and are summed up in it. The first generation of Christians was not yet capable of writing a creed like that. But they did already possess the two elements which make up its basic framework: the actions of Jesus and the summary of the whole plan, history, and mystery of salvation in the three Persons of God. When they first united the two in one explicit formula no one can say — the evidence is lacking. But where it probably took place we can easily guess. They must first have united them in connection with baptism.

What makes this almost certain? First, the fact of Matthew's baptismal formula: "baptize them in the name of the Father and of the Son and of the Holy Spirit." This is, we have been saying, the divine plan of salvation, as sketched for example in the opening hymn of Ephesians:

> . . . God and Father of our Lord Jesus Christ, who in Christ has blessed us . . . chosen us . . . out of love predestined us. . . .
> In him [Jesus] we have our redemption through his blood, the remission of our transgressions. . . .
> . . . have been sealed with the promised Holy Spirit, who is the first installment of our inheritance (Eph 1, 3–14).

But it is also baptism in which we "have been baptized into

union with Christ's death. We were buried with him by means of Baptism, in order that, just as Christ was raised from the dead by the glorious power of the Father, so we . . ." (Rom 6, 3–4). But this being baptized "into" the death of Jesus is also in the same passage referred to as being "baptized into Jesus"; and it indicates the same reality as is expressed so often in the Acts and epistles with the words "baptized in [into] the name of Jesus." Baptism could be referred to in either of the two formulas: baptizing in the name of the Father, the Son, and the Holy Spirit, or baptizing in the name of Jesus. Why? Because each refers to a different aspect of the one salvific reality — first, as it was worked out in Christ; second, as it expresses the work of the three divine Persons, across (and before and after) history. Perhaps the Trinitarian formula and the death-and-resurrection formula were already united when these New Testament works were written. But if not, they stood side by side as formulas connected with baptism; they stood side by side as explanations of the Christian message; and the fullness of truth and perfection of expression is reached when they are blended together as in our creeds.

❖　　❖　　❖

One simple and short way to present the whole message in a very small nutshell is the beloved expression of St. Paul, "in Christ" or "in Christ Jesus." These phrases and similar ones occur again and again in his letters in every imaginable situation. They drive home the point that to him "to live is Christ" and "Christ in you" is "your hope of glory." They sum up the New Testament reality, the good news, which is the reality of Christ — Jesus who has been sent by God to suffer, die, and rise from the dead to eternal glory — and our share in him and through him in all that he stands for.

❖　　❖　　❖

This last-noted formulation, "in Christ," takes us to another simple capsule summary of the whole message. This final summary formula will give us what is really the best possible answer to the question from which we began, "what is this good news?" For we have seen that the good news is the reality of all the truths we have been outlining so far, and more. It is the fulfilling of the old prophecies and hopes of Israel in Jesus, it is the salvation of all the peoples of the world if they will but believe in this Jesus the Christ. The good news is the summary of all things which happened to Christ, and it is the announcement that we are able to share in all of these. It is then too the summary of the acts and the virtues by which we enter into the new life in Christ, and especially of the reality which is that gift of his Spirit. And it is all the consequences of possessing that Spirit here below: the life in the Church in union and love and in patient endurance, filling up the sufferings of Christ for his Body the Church; and the continual resurrection from day to day, the daily triumph experienced in ourselves over sin and suffering and death. And the good news is the forgiveness of sins, and the resurrection of the body and life eternal in the world to come, and all of this in Christ. The good news is the love of God for us, the long and carefully planned salvation God has wrought for us in Christ. And of course the good news is also all the experienced consequences of our life of faith in these things — truth, light, joy, peace, and the union with the presence of Christ. The good news is, in brief, the fact that we are saved in Jesus dying on the cross for love of us, and all the consequences that flow therefrom.

Therefore the writers of the New Testament had a still briefer and still more complete formula for all this than any we have examined so far. It occurs in connection with the Greek word "to preach the good news, to evangelize," which, if translated exactly into English would be "to good-news-ize." For the New Testament speaks not only of good-news-izing about Christ, or of good-news-izing the facts or the truth or the faith. Several times it uses the expression "to good-news-ize Christ Jesus" — that is, in normal English, to preach Christ Jesus, where Christ or Jesus stands simply for "the gospel, the good news."

This fits in too with a usage that runs through the whole New Testament, a certain play on words, where Christ, the Person himself, is spoken of as God's Word. This usage is found not only in the well-known texts of St. John — "The Word was made flesh and dwelt among us" and "In the beginning was the Word" (which have a deeper meaning as well) but is also alluded to in statements like St. Paul's "The Son of that God, Jesus Christ, who was preached among you through our instrumentality, mine, Sylvanus', and Timothy's, did not prove to be Yes and No, but in him was realized the Yes. In fact, whatever God promised finds its yes in him, and for that reason we say the Amen through him to God's glory" (2 Cor 1, 19–20). The word which is Christ is Yes, is Amen.

There are many others, sometimes it is not certain how to interpret them — "The word of God" is preached, dwells in the heart, shows strength and power, etc. There is good reason to think in many of these cases that "Christ" could easily be substituted, was actually in the authors' minds, when they wrote "word."

At any rate, in regard to "gospel" it is certain. The best and most accurate summary statement of the good news is the identification: Christ Jesus is the good news. He embodies in his own Person all the facts on which the preaching is based, all the possibilities of men's participating in those facts, he is the salvation itself begun and consummated, he is the "Alpha and the Omega, the Beginning and the End," who "was and who is and who is to come." One can explain and explain without end what propositions are contained in, implied in, and necessarily presupposed by the good news. In fact one must keep trying to do so. But all the time, in the real Church of every day, and in the life of many fervent Christians, the still deeper reality is known, touched, lived, felt. Christ is the good news. And this is not poetry, not rhetoric, not imagination. This is the deepest truth of the New Testament. And this will be finally the foundation stone of our scientific understanding in Chapter 13 of what the four written gospels really are.

What Is a Gospel?

EVERYTHING we have seen in the preceding chapters and much more besides had to be passed on and explained to each new convert.

An organized instruction in the basic implications of the kerygma was needed in order to introduce the neophyte into what was an already existing community. One could not simply make an act of faith and be done with it. True, the Holy Spirit came to the baptized in a special way at the imposition of hands. True, in this, the Messianic age, "they shall all be taught of God" and "will have no need that any man shall teach you." And yet, no one enters in one moment into the full perfection of the Messianic age and its highest possibilities of charismatic living. One grows up into it, grows up in Christ, each one as an individual and the community as a whole, and the individual does so within the community, and controlled, guided, measured by the community.

So we find that from the first the early Christians could not and did not simply "let themselves go" in the Spirit. Or where certain groups tried to do so, they soon fell into excesses and disorders, and had to be called to task and set straight. Rather, they began their Christian lives with at least some basic organized instruction in what the kerygma really meant and really implied, and what its consequences — at least basically and in summary form — for their lives really were. And then, in the community, they set about living according to "the teaching of the apostles."

Moreover, because the Christians lived as a community, traditions grew up among them as to how things should be done, traditional ways of thinking and acting, traditional ways of presenting and explaining the central truths. When problems and questions arose about how to live their Christian life, they took them to the leaders of the community. Solutions became rules of life in many cases, fixed patterns were found, tried, standardized, regularized, applied. And fixed forms of instruction were worked out to pass on these things too — instructions adapted to their own special needs and problems.

All of this had to be. The epistles give evidence for it, but reason alone makes it clear that it must have been so. This is the way people live. And this is, as we saw, one of the main human reasons for having a community, a Church. It is in the long run the only way of assuring that people shall continue to be able to experience and to live out the good news in practice.

Now the good news may be summarized in one word as "Christ." They knew this too. They had experienced it. And so it was perfectly natural that in looking for answers to problems and trying to work out in detail how the cross-resurrection pattern should be lived in day-to-day reality, they should look first and above all to the teachings and the words and the actions, the living example of Christ. True, often enough even the apostles had not understood him at the time he first spoke. "Kingdom of God" in his mind and in theirs were quite different realities. And when he talked of Messianic sufferings, of death-resurrection, and even when he referred, according to their capacity, to his own utterly singular relation with God, he still seems to have spoken right over their heads. The gospel stories warn us again and again that the apostles did not understand these things as they were spoken to them by Jesus.

How then could they apply his teachings, words, and acts to their own problems now if they had not understood them at the time they heard? They could do so because between then and now they had experienced Jesus' dying and had seen him risen and glorified, and they had received the gift and the illumination of the Holy Spirit. Now they could understand. Now everything fell into place. Now they could see what he had meant all along. And now they could see in every treasured word of his which they recollected a deeper meaning than they had perhaps even suspected before. Christ's words, as they recalled them now, glowed with meaning, a meaning that bore directly on this their Christian daily living. They had not been able to see it when they first heard the word, because they did not yet possess that which was the heart and essence of Christian living — the experience of the dying-rising Jesus and the insight of the Holy Spirit into him. But now they possessed them, and now they could see how his meaning was perfectly applicable, was just what they needed to settle their wondering what this new life was all about, which way they should go next, how they were to console and encourage, teach and exhort. And so the apostles used these things in their teaching. They used them in answering problems, even new problems. And the community lived by them.

For instance, take one of Jesus' miracles of healing. At the time they saw it, it was a work of mercy perhaps or of power, at the most a divine testimony to Christ's word. But looking at it now, they could see how it contained the gospel message in miniature. They could see in it that Jesus had been living and preaching the gospel message all the time they knew him, long before they themselves had grasped what that message was. A poor sufferer comes to Jesus, admits his own misery and helplessness, expresses faith in Jesus as his only hope, as God's appointed means of healing; and, contrary to all one would naturally expect, he finds his life transformed, his ailment done away with, his sin and his sickness left behind, and himself in a new relation to his fellowmen.

They would tell a story like that, using the words "to save" on two or three levels of meaning simultaneously, showing in the accompanying circumstances or words the relation of sin to human misery, stressing any action of Jesus reminiscent of the Christian sacraments, noting that the healing or salvation came finally through touching Jesus or being touched by him (levels of meaning again: spiritual, physical, sacramental, etc.), or through believing his word.

It was not mere ingenuity that enabled the Patristic commentators to find whole chains of allegorical meanings relative to the great mysteries of the Christian life in some of these stories. Ingenious they often were. But often too there is a real foundation in the story itself for drawing out references to baptism, faith, contrasts with the Old Law, obedience and humility, love of the neighbor, etc. For as these events from Jesus' life were told and used in Christian preaching and teaching, they were shaped to the purpose, unessential details were dropped, significant ones were retained, heightened, and even completed where necessary with the addition of details from other stories, etc. Thus was made more and more clear the meaning and model of the Christian's life in Christ, in a set way of teaching which depended completely on the stories and words of Jesus as remembered and passed on by the responsible members of the community.

Again, to the believing Christian, the things Jesus had done could never have been mere wonders such as could have been told of any charlatan or wandering Oriental magician (Acts 8, 9–11; Mt 12, 27). This was Jesus, Savior, God among us. Thus when they recalled that he cleansed a leper with a word, they saw this at once in the light of their own cleansing from sin as they had experienced it when they themselves came to him crying for a cure and ready to do whatever he commanded as God's way of salvation.

Again, for them, in faith, the world had been transformed. All is made clear: why life is so frustrating at times, why we must suffer and die, what life is all about. The world is tinted with a new light, and they know the light comes from faith. Their eyes have been opened. And now they hear the story of Jesus' opening the eyes of a man born blind. . . . They could not, they did not fail to make the connection.

And consequently they tell these stories in a special way, a way adapted to bringing out the teaching value that was in them from the day the events themselves occurred. Sometimes it happened among different groups that the same incident would be recounted in slightly different ways. The basic fact would remain the same, perhaps even the moral drawn from it. But physical details would vary. Or again, a single saying of our Lord would be so rich in meaning that it could be used to bring out different points in different contexts. So it was.

Some stories brought out the dispositions needed to approach Christ and find salvation in him. Some stressed the deeper truths about this Lord of theirs — his divine power, the love with which he gave himself for men. Some brought out truths about the Church, the Body of Christ on earth, its contrast with the old order of Judaism, the universality of salvation, etc. Sometimes a word or action of Christ had no clearly recognizable applicable meaning. For these an applicable meaning would be sought, as it has been in every age. These are the normal processes of Christian preaching and teaching.

From an early date these stories and sayings began to be collected into groups, sometimes according to the nature of the intrinsic subject matter, sometimes according to the special needs of the people who were going to use them or the occasion for which they were to be used. It is to some such groupings that Luke refers at the beginning of his gospel: "Many an attempt has been made before now to present the drama of events that have come to a climax among us, so as to accord with the tradition which the original eyewitnesses and ministers of the gospel have handed down to us" (Lk 1, 1–2).

All these instructions centered on Jesus. He is the gospel. And the answering of problems too centered on Jesus for the same reason. It follows that if they assembled them all together into a single manual, a single "textbook of dogmatic, moral, and ascetical and liturgical theology," it would all center on Jesus, all be drawn directly from his words, acts, teachings, illustrated by his example. Conversely, if they were to write or relate the life of Jesus, putting together all these stories and words which they had preserved, the resulting life would tend to be at the same time something of a collection of all the moral, ascetic, dogmatic, liturgical, controversial teachings. For the life of Jesus, as they told it in all these individual stories, already either contained all or pointed toward all these things.

*　　*　　*

And now we are ready to ask, What is a gospel? for we have seen all the elements which go to make one up. The first essential element in the definition of a gospel is this: each of the four individual gospels is first of all "the gospel." Each of them is the good news, the message; the same one that we analyzed especially in the first chapters of the book. The gospel which we found in every one of the apostolic sermons contained a handful of fundamental elements: Jesus is God's chosen and anointed representative; Jesus lived a perfectly holy life, the life of the just man and prophet, teaching and doing good in God's name; Jesus was unjustly rejected by his people, condemned and put to death; Jesus accepted this willingly, knowingly, deliberately, for the good of the people and for all men and in submission to God's will for him; Jesus rose from the dead and is in glory with God. All this was foretold by the prophets. And now man's salvation is in believing this word from God.

But this lineup of elements we recognize as the basic outline of any one of the four gospels. It is important to be clear on this point. These are not just things one happens to find in the four gospels. They are what a gospel *is*.

The central point is of course the salvific events themselves, the passion and the resurrection. The direct proclamation of the significance of these events is made by our Lord or an angel in the resurrection appearances. And the pointing out of Jesus as a holy one, and *the* Holy One of God is expanded into a whole long story, a connected series of incidents from the public life of Jesus. His acceptance is above all in the supper and garden accounts. Apart from that, the individual evangelists can and do weave one or more of these five elements through and into many other parts of their story according to their own purposes and designs, as we shall see further on.

The first step in understanding the gospels and seeing what they really are is to realize that their aim is to proclaim, to spell out clearly this message, this basic lineup of facts which they, the writer or the apostle on whom he based himself, had seen and was willing to bear witness to unto death if necessary. And this is the first element too in judging the "historicity," "reliability," etc., of the gospel accounts.

It has become a common place to say that the gospels were not intended to be history books, not intended to be "biographies" in the modern sense. But, true as this is, it must not lead us to forget that they do intend to bear historical witness to something that happened, something which they know and affirm is a fact — the death and resurrection of Jesus. This is the very point of their being written in the first place. This is the most important and central fact about what a gospel *is*. The supreme application of the modern critical principle of determining the literary genre of any given piece of writing before judging its historical value is soundly made here by recognizing that the gospel, a gospel, is first of all and above all a witness to the fact that this good news is true.

That is the meaning of Luke's prologue: "that you should appreciate the certainty of the oral instruction you have already received . . ." (Lk 1, 4); of Mark's: "A summary of the gospel of Jesus Christ, the Son of God" (Mk 1, 1). This is what St. John writes: "This much . . . has been recorded that you may persevere in your belief that Jesus is the Messias, the Son of God, and that through your belief, you may have life in his name" (Jn 20, 31).

The first thing to be gotten out of a reading of any gospel is precisely that message. If we have not grasped that aspect of the gospels yet, then the best thing to do at this point is to take one of them in hand at once and read it through, looking precisely for this outline. At least once every Christian should have gone through the gospel looking for, getting the feel of, its central proclamation, not letting himself be distracted by pharisees and publicans or turned aside even to admire the magnificent details of the moral example and sublime teaching of Jesus. He should read the whole story, seeing it as a simple expansion of, e.g., Acts 10, 36–43 (Peter's instruction of Cornelius). At least once one should have tried to read it, getting the full sweep of its powerful story, letting things fall into place according to that simple outline.

One finds that a gospel is above all the passion story ("we preach Christ crucified"), and that is why so large a part of each gospel is taken up with recounting the last hours of Jesus' life. But the passion and death do not stand without the resurrection, and the sending of the apostles to preach the meaning of this event to the world, and so another disproportionately long section is given to the appearances of the risen Christ. These two make up the essence of the story. It is prepared for with the long supper and garden accounts, which bring out Christ's willing, loving, obedient acceptance of this and his call for the disciples' participation in it in the future. And that is introduced by a dramatization of Christ's rejection by the people, in a series of confrontations with the leaders of the people in Jerusalem, and pronouncement of final doom on those who will not accept God's offered salvation.

What we have just sketched takes up easily half the gospel accounts in the synoptics, though it has to do only with the last few days of Jesus' life. What precedes it is an expansion of the points implied in the kerygmatic announcement "he went about doing good," and an attempt to identify in various ways who and what this key figure, this Jesus was, as in the announcement: "God's chosen one, God's Sent," etc. Thus all the gospels begin their active, adult story with the preaching of John the Baptist and his testimony to Jesus. (The infancy narratives of Matthew and Luke and the Logos hymn of John are prologues of the gospel. Style and manner of treatment clearly mark those prologues off from the rest of the story.) In the same way, the sermon in Acts says "beginning from Galilee, after the baptism which John preached" and the apostolic community in Acts 1, seeking someone to take the place of Judas the traitor, sought among "the men who have accompanied us during all the time that the Lord Jesus went in and out among us, beginning from the Baptism of John."

✽   ✽   ✽

The second element in a written gospel has to do with the

presuppositions and consequences of the preached good news; that is, with all the things we described in Chapters 5 to 11. We saw at the beginning of this chapter how these things, as much as the message of salvation itself, were taught and explained and worked out in all the early preaching and teaching in terms of Jesus himself. They were based on words and works from his life as the apostles who had witnessed and heard these words and works recounted them and understood them, now that they had been enlightened by the Holy Spirit and by the crowning experience of his death and resurrection.

We concluded that they could hardly speak of these truths, without constant reference to Jesus, just as they could hardly speak of Jesus without constant reference to the actual significance and fullness of meaning which all his life and actions and words had assumed for them now. It is this process which culminates in the second element in the written gospels.

To understand this, we could start from either of two points of view: the gospels as we know them or the preaching of the good news. If we start with the gospels, we ask, after acknowledging the first essential element in them, What about all these other things which are obviously in the gospels? The message, the good news, can be summed up in a few words, as we see in the sermons in Acts. What then are all those many, many other details which we find in the gospels, over and above this essential element? Why are they there?

A good and easy answer would be, of course, that they are there simply because that is the way things actually happened. Jesus' words are there simply because he actually spoke them, his teachings are there simply because these are the things which he most tried to impress upon his apostles.

The answer is good, but it is inadequate. It raises most of the problems we mentioned in Chapter 1. For instance, it leaves us asking, Why these details and not others? It does not tell us why, out of all the thousands and thousands of incidents, thousands of sayings uttered, thousands of people cured, the evangelists chose out just the few that they did choose. It does not begin to make clear to us why, in writing four very brief little accounts which are our only record of those thousands of precious happenings — "Other things also Jesus did, so many that if they were written down the world itself I think would not suffice to contain so many books" (Jn 21, 25) — why, when each of four men is choosing forty or fifty incidents out of so rich a stock of possibilities, a few hundred words out of what must have been an enormous treasury of sayings of our Lord — why, in these four accounts, over and above the basic outline of the essential kerygma, there should be so very much repetition and overlapping.

Again, to say that the details over and above the kerygma as such are there only to satisfy our desire to know what happened, does not account for the fact of divergences and differences between the accounts of the same incidents in various gospels — differences which frequently cannot (reasonably) be harmonized with one another.

Nor does it explain facts like the same saying of Jesus appearing in different contexts and with different meanings, the order of incidents being changed from gospel to gospel, the differences in time and place between the Synoptics and John, and many similar things.

No, the question, Why so many other details over and above the message itself? receives only the beginning of an answer from the fact that they are in the gospels because they actually happened. That is far from the whole explanation.

Another way of approaching this second element in the construction of a gospel would be to start with the teaching, fragments of which we drew from the epistles in Chapters 5 to 11. If the gospels represent, as tradition says, the teaching and preaching of the apostles, should they not present, besides the kerygma itself, something of all these explanations and clarifications? Not only the good news, but also its implications and consequences?

Here fit the rest of the problems we listed in Chapter 1: for, looking at the written gospels, we ask, Where are these applications? Where are the conclusions for practical daily life? Where are the theological explanations? Where are the moral exhortations? Such things must have made up part of the apostolic preaching. Are they lacking in the gospels, which supposedly sum up that preaching?

The gospel outline gives us the central and largest portion of our creed. But to explain why and how this creed and this gospel sums up our salvation, we must advance from creed to catechism, to Christian doctrine. Who was Jesus that his death and resurrection should be so important for us? What must we do to obtain the full effects of his dying and rising? These things make up not only the catechism of today. More deeply probed, more scientifically analyzed, they also make up today's dogmatic and moral theology. But this too could not have been, in fact obviously was not, lacking in the primitive Church. Was it never summed up anywhere?

Of course it was. It was summed up in the kind of accounts we spoke of above, accounts in the ordinary teaching and preaching which taught and illustrated doctrine and practice by the details and the words from the life of Jesus, the Lord, and which recounted incidents and sayings from the life of Jesus, in order to give knowledge of him, to edify, instruct and exhort through his word and example the rest of the community.

Of all his words and all his works, those would have most chance of living on which had made the deepest impression on those present at the time they happened; second, those which now, looking back in the light of what they had learned about Jesus, they could see were most expressive of who and what he was and of what he was going to do for them and through them; and, third, those which the simple facts of daily life would give them the most occasion to recall often. This last, of course, varied according to their circumstances, but would include for instance his teachings on the passing away of the old religious order, on the likelihood of persecutions, etc.

At any rate, collections of these incidents and sayings from the life of Christ grew up, and were used as needed by the individual preachers. They did not grow up haphazardly, but according to the needs and therefore under the direction of the living Church.

The inexhaustible sources for the facts, stories, sayings, and teachings needed were of course those who had known Jesus personally, especially the apostles. And each preacher recounted at length the central incident, the passion story with its accompanying introductory material and its conclusion in triumph and glory.

Put these two together and one gets a written gospel as we know it today. The basic outline is the kerygma. We saw that above. The rest of it is a collection of these stories and sayings which the apostles remembered and passed on from the life of Christ as they had experienced it. Each little paragraph of this life contains some point of its own, some message, some doctrine. All strung together, in a way which will fit the basic outline and pattern of the kerygma, and which will reflect also in rough outline the general movements of Jesus' life — contact with John the Baptist, preaching in Galilee, movement toward Jerusalem, etc. — they give us what is for all practical purposes a life of Jesus.

We ask at once, Is it a biography of Jesus or is it a manual of Christian doctrine? The answer is hard to give. It is both. Our categories of thought distinguish the two. But as we saw above, as regards this unique case of the Christ, the early Christians' categories would hardly leave room for the distinction. Jesus is all and in all. Every point of doctrine and practice derives from him, his life, his sayings. And all of his life is filled with meaning and value for doctrine and for practice. The result of arranging all these illustrative and exhortative incidents together in a framework which does correspond to the great periods of his life and which above all fits within the basic good news message is a completely special, a unique literary form — the gospel. It is neither biography, nor theology, but somehow both at once, because to the minds of those Christians, when it comes to this singular, unique case of Jesus, the two tend to be one. "In him are all treasures of wisdom and knowledge," "to know him and the fellowship of his sufferings," "to know him and to be found in him," "to know the great mystery of the divine plan for mankind, that mystery which is Christ in you and your hope of glory" — these are their typical expressions for grasp of the Christian message and growth in it, for fuller and fuller mastery of all it means and stands for in knowledge and in action. "To me to live is Christ." "I preach Christ crucified, Christ the wisdom of God and the power of God."

So this is the second point, the second constituent element of a written gospel: the fleshing out of the skeleton outline with narratives of what "Jesus began to do and to teach"; expanding especially that point in the outline message which said Jesus "went about doing good and healing all that were oppressed by the devil, for God was with him." These stories are arranged according to the general outline of "the word which was proclaimed throughout all Judea, beginning from Galilee after the baptism which John preached." These narratives are written from four different points of view, as we shall try to explain next under the third constituent element of the gospel form. They differ in details within some of the stories, details in the exact expression of a saying, details of the order of the events within the larger outline. But their purpose never was to communicate these details for their own sake. The point of these stories and sayings is the Christian life and teaching as it is summed up in Jesus' real life in this world, as the apostles knew it and taught it to the Christian communities of their time. Each bears its point, its meaning and message. And that meaning and message rarely depends on a detail of time, place, accompaniment; it rarely depends on a single turn of phrase. Where it does, there are no conflicts.

So each of these little accounts or sayings or discourses has its own point and message, which flows from or leads to the gospel as such, the kerygma, the communication of which in its fullness is the point of the gospels as a whole.

Some examples? We shall see a few in the following chapter. It is important to notice here however that though the principle just explained as to what most of these accounts originally were is generally accepted today, there is considerable uncertainty about the exact point of each individual section. Classifications of them differ from author to author. And further and more careful examination of the full background of these stories in the current literature of that time and especially in the Old Testament continues to turn up new possibilities of deeper implied and sometimes hidden meanings.

*   ○   ○

The third element is something we referred to above when we mentioned some further cause for their being four written gospels instead of only one. We summed it up there as four different viewpoints. That was however too hasty a summary, and needs expansion and explanation now.

The work of an evangelist was to gather these points of teaching from the life of Jesus as they existed in the Church, in the teaching and preaching of the apostles above all, and make a single story out of them. To do this, simple collecting was not enough; at least it was not looked on as enough by our four evangelists, whatever may have been the case of others whose work was rejected by the Church and died out. The evangelists had to gather this material in terms of a special theme of their own. This theme, this individual viewpoint, was that of a theologian-historian or historian-theologian, with emphasis on one aspect or the other, varying according to personalities and divine inspiration. This theme was some essential aspect of the basic gospel or good news: how the gospel, the salvific events, Christ, is the replacing of the old order by the new, for example — if that is an adequate statement of St. Matthew's intention.

But here we may as well admit the difficulty from the first. While exegetes generally admit that each evangelist had a theme, a definite theological point of view, some one aspect of the great message which he was trying to stress, and that the events and sayings each narrates are chosen and to a large extent arranged in conformity with that theme, there is not yet complete agreement by any means as to what the individual themes of the different evangelists are. According as one exegete or another sees a different theme as outstanding, he is likely to discover a different outline in the gospel he is working on; or again often enough, beginning with a different outline, seemingly imposed by the order of events or by key words, exegetes may come up with convictions of different basic themes. This too is one of the fields receiving most attention these days: just what exact point was each of the evangelists making, and how does each one's outline and order and selection and variation in details serve his special end?

At any rate, exegetes are agreed on the need to look for each gospel's own principle of arrangement and selection, each one's own central theme. It is something over and above the general basic theme essential to being a gospel, over and above the good news, the salvific fact of Jesus. It is also something over and above the general factual outline of a Galilean and a Judean ministry, climaxing finally in Jerusalem. It is rather an individual approach to the salvific fact, an individual way of presenting the meaning and the consequences of the gospel. It is bringing out one certain fundamental aspect of the message, as much as possible all the way through the rest of the account. We shall see some examples in Chapter 14.

So these are the three elements of which we can, so far at least, speak with some confidence as making up a written gospel. There is a fourth, but it is out of our hands, and perhaps undiscoverable. That is the divine intention in arranging things just this way, in seeing that these four aspects should complement one another in just the way God intended for the good of future ages. Not, to be sure, to give men every biographical detail they would desire about the life of Jesus — far from that. But to see that they could get, by continual meditation on the gospels in the Church, a full basic picture of all that is implied in this good news.

CHAPTER 14

For Instance, St. Mark

LET us look at a few examples of the main points mentioned
in the past chapter. The gospel according to St. Mark is the
shortest of the four gospels. Superficially at least, it can impress
a reader as a simple and naïve, practically artless account of
random events in the life of Jesus. From Mark many modern
historians (with the help of scissors and paste, to be sure) have
built up their picture of Jesus the apocalyptic preacher and faith
healer. Mark will be a good example for us of how a gospel
presents theology through the life of Christ.

Unfortunately, we cannot continue in this chapter the practice
of printing the full text every time we refer to the Bible. If the
following examples then are to be clear the reader must have
a copy of the gospel according to St. Mark in his hand from the
beginning and keep referring to it constantly during the course
of the exposition.

We said in the past chapter that the first thing to be looked
for in a gospel is precisely the presentation of "the gospel." We
saw that the gospel writer wishes, like the first preachers, to be
taken as a witness to the fact that a certain set of events really
happened. Those events are the passion, death, and resurrection
of Jesus Christ. Mark wishes to affirm the reality of these events.
For they are "the gospel." On them hangs all that the Christian
message is, all that the Christian life consists in. On them depends
the Christian hope.

In presenting this "gospel," he follows the outline of the

message about Christ that we have been studying from the beginning. There is first the coming of John the Baptist, his preaching, and the witness which he bears to Christ (1, 1–8). This climaxes in the baptism of Jesus himself, and God's testimony to him (1, 9–13). Then follows an expanded account of Jesus' activity, of how he began "to do and to preach," performing works which marked him out as being truly God's representative. His own words and the words of others identify him as the longed-for Messiah, the hope of Israel. And his preaching and his action both work to destroy sin and the whole kingdom of evil (1, 13–8, 26).

Still further proof is given that Jesus' career is being lived out according to God's design and purpose: from 8, 27 on, Jesus, having gained from the apostles some basic understanding and recognition of his mission as Messiah, goes on to teach them in considerable detail how this mission will be accomplished, his own destiny of suffering, death, and resurrection (8, 27–10, 45).

Chapters 11 and 12 of Mark are devoted especially and almost exclusively to a point-by-point dramatization of the fact that Israel, especially Israel's leaders and the various parties and groups which made up the active political and religious life of Israel in those days, all rejected Christ. Mark 13 elaborates on the fact that God was about to reject Israel, that the old order would pass, be destroyed, and the days of the Son of Man come in their place.

Mark 14 and 15 are the passion story itself. Two prologues — the supper and the garden — mark out unmistakably the divine intention and purpose and Christ's deliberate acceptance of it. At the end of Chapter 15 Christ dies under the eyes of witnesses, and is buried — again under the eyes of witnesses, who are carefully named and noted, and after official confirmation of the fact of his death.

Chapter 16 tells of the fact of his resurrection; the finding of the empty tomb and the vision of an angel who announces that Jesus is risen and that he will appear to the disciples and to Peter in Galilee. Verses 9–20 of this chapter sum up several appearances of the risen Jesus and his final commission to the apostles to preach everywhere in his name, working signs, healing the sick, demanding faith. And finally Jesus was taken to the right hand of God, whence he assisted their work on earth.

(These last verses [9 to 20], though not usually considered the work of St. Mark himself, do serve to fill out the format which the Church recognized a gospel should have. Some think the verses were added to an original gospel which ended with verse 8, others that they simply replace in summary form a somewhat longer original ending of Mark's. Either way, verses 1 to 8 already contain the divine announcement [by the angel] of the resurrection, and the physical witness to the empty tomb by the very witnesses who had seen Christ die and who had seen his dead body laid in this tomb and sealed in by a very large stone which three women together could not move from the doorway.)

This is the heart and essence of the gospel, the direct recounting of the Christ-event, following the basic outline and making very clear the basic points of the preached message.

The second element in the composition of a gospel is, we have said, the explanation of what the death and resurrection of the Messiah mean for us. It contains the explanations of suffering, persecution, sacrifice, and of love and service, and shows that they necessarily flow from a right interpretation of what happens to Jesus. There will also be an account of how the Church results from Jesus' acts and is men's way of participating in them. And from this will be shown to result other basic changes in the God-man relationship — consequences for the liturgical life, changed attitudes toward the law and traditions of Israel, a new understanding of the Old Testament. There will be explanations of the reality of redemption itself: conquest of sin, of disease, of all powers outside of God and opposed to God. There will be, moreover, "dogmatic" teachings, which the good news presupposes and which give it its value and meaning: the Trinity, the Incarnation, the need of redemption.

All of these explanations and lessons will be given in and through the Lord's own words and actions, as these were remembered by those who had known him personally, and as they were applied to the needs of the Church by the Church's own leaders and teachers in their active tradition of teaching and of preaching.

An instance of this kind of teaching is found in Mark 7, 24–30. The paragraph begins: "Jesus now left that place and set out for the district of Tyre and Sidon." What "that place" is, is not specified, either here or earlier. Jesus is somewhere in Galilee, but we are not told where. The goal of the trip is clear however: the region of the two famous pagan cities of Tyre and Sidon, often used in the Old Testament as examples of the might and pride of the Gentile world.

The journey is a major one, about fifty or sixty miles at least. Up to this point, Mark has shown Jesus preaching only around the little Lake of Genesareth (some thirteen miles by eight miles at its widest points) and once "through the length and breadth of Galilee" (about fifty miles by twenty-five miles at its longest and broadest points). This journey, however, takes Jesus to a region well outside of his home province and into completely pagan territory, the country of the Phoenicians.

Still, in the gospel account, there is no discussion or planning of the journey ahead of time, nor is there a description of what happened or what was seen along the way. In 7, 23, Jesus is finishing a conversation with the disciples in a house somewhere in Galilee: "'. . . fraud, wantonness, envy, profanity, pride, folly. All these wicked things come from within and defile a person.' And rising up from that place, he went off to the district of Tyre and Sidon." Simply that.

Once arrived, "he went indoors and wanted no one to know of it." But a woman heard he was there, and came to implore a favor of him. Jesus speaks one sentence to her, she answers in one sentence, Jesus grants the favor. "He then left the district of Tyre and went, by way of Sidon, to the Sea of Galilee, down through the heart of the Decapolis"; that is, he made a circle back toward his starting point, another journey by foot of sixty to ninety miles. Mark tells nothing of what happened on this journey either until he is "in the heart of the Decapolis," near the journey's end.

The biographies of Jesus written in recent centuries by Catholics and non-Catholics alike find this kind of reporting intolerable. Therefore they add to it discussions of why Jesus made this journey, why at this time, where exactly he started from, who went with him, where he stayed at the end, how he found the house he stayed in, how long he stayed there, how the woman heard of him, how he passed his time, why he decided to return, why he took the different route back, etc. For these things are the stuff of biography. And no ordinary biography can relate calmly that its hero finished speaking a sentence, rose up and walked sixty miles, then held a short conversation, and began an eighty-mile walk back.

But the gospel of Mark is not an ordinary biography. Church tradition before Mark wrote had preserved the account of a certain conversation with a native of the region of Tyre and Sidon, "a Greek-speaking heathen, a Syrophoenician by birth." The conversation had been of great importance for clarifying the teaching of Jesus and for justifying the practice of the apostolic Church. Mark records that conversation, perhaps even in the very words in which he heard it from St. Peter. Practically all other details concerning the incident have dropped away.

Those which remain are necessary to bring the conversation into being and give it a point. It needs a location, not an exact one, but at least one clearly in pagan territory. It needs characters — the woman, as pagan as can be. It needs an occasion and an external sign — the possessed daughter to be healed. But the rest, all that we called "the very stuff of biography," and which the modern biographers of Christ are at such pains to supply, was not necessary and, as far as we have evidence, was not regularly recounted in the early preaching and teaching which Mark's gospel summarizes.

What is so important about the conversation?

She implored him to drive the demon out of her daughter. He said to her: "Let first the children have their fill; it surely is not

fair to take the children's bread and throw it to the dogs." "You
are right, sir," she promptly assented; "and the dogs under the
table eat of the crumbs of the children's bread." "For that
remark," he said to her, "you may go home. The demon is driven
out of your daughter" (7, 26–29).

The children are the Jews. The "dogs" are people like her,
non-Jews, pagans, outsiders. The "bread" is what Jesus has to
offer, his good works — here a healing in her favor — and then
all that goes with them. She wins her request with the answer
she gives to Jesus' harsh rebuff. She and those like her, she says,
will be content with the leavings of the children's bread, the simple
crumbs that fall to the floor.

What does it mean? We have seen the long disputes in the
early Church over how the Gentiles were to find salvation in
Christ, when the whole Old Testament had seemed to direct its
promises to the Jews. Words of Jesus like "I am not sent but to
the lost sheep of the house of Israel" and "Go not into the ways
of the Gentiles" were quoted by the rigorist party in the Church.
But the full doctrine was that of Paul's summary in Romans:
"The gospel is God's salvation to them that believe, to Jew first
and then to Greek" (Rom 1, 16). And over and over in the Acts
of the Apostles, we see how the early Church lived by this principle, turning first to the Jewish community in any new region
where missionaries entered, and then when these rejected the
message, turning to the Gentiles.

This little conversation and story is a perfect exposition of
that truth and that way of acting. "Salvation is from the Jews."
But "Very well, since you will not believe, henceforth I will turn
to the Gentiles." This is not some pious application of the story.
This is the literal meaning of the words. The woman says the
Gentiles have a right to what the Jews have left. Jesus accepts
the principle. He does so only in a private conversation and in
this one individual case, true. But the Church used this conversation and this case as representative of his general attitude
and teaching. He had not himself gone out to preach regularly
among the Gentiles. He had not during his lifetime sent the

apostles to do so either. But the Gentile world receives what the Jews left. And in practice, the Jews left almost everything.

Thus the woman speaks only of crumbs, but what actually follows in Mark's story? Jesus goes to the heart of the Decapolis, still Gentile territory, and the people "went beyond all bounds in expressing their delight." In that same territory, after three days of teaching the people, Jesus multiplies seven loaves of bread and feeds four thousand men.

Now this multiplication of bread in Gentile territory is the second miraculous feeding Mark has related. The first one was in Jewish territory and for the Jews. The numbers involved in the two feedings seem, according to recent analyses, deliberately symbolic: the Jewish group was fed, as David had been, with five loaves from the twelve sacred loaves which were always before the Lord (Mk 2, 25-26; Lev 24, 5-9). The Gentiles were fed with the seven which the Jews had not taken. The fragments of the Jewish feeding filled twelve baskets, one for each of the tribes of Israel. The fragments of the Gentile feeding filled seven baskets, for the traditional seventy nations of the Gentiles (Gn 10) (just as later seven deacons with Greek names would be appointed to see that the Greek-speaking Hellenists were not neglected — Acts 6, 1-6).

Both miraculous feedings, when Jesus gave bread to the Jews as well as when he gave it to the Gentiles, are told in such a way as to bring out their resemblances to the Christian Eucharist: "Taking the loaves into his hands, he looked up to heaven, and said grace over them, and broke them into portions, which he gave to his disciples to distribute to the crowd." The Gentiles receive what the Jews leave — bread in abundance. And, along with Jewish believers and on an equal basis with them, the Gentiles will be fed with the Body of Christ.

Between the two feedings occurred the incident of the Syrophoenician woman of Tyre and Sidon. It was a remembrance of Jesus preserved in the Christian preaching and teaching. But it was preserved not for the journey itself — of which nothing is said; nor for his stay in Tyre — which is not described; nor to describe a particularly striking miracle — for he had cast out hundreds of demons. It was preserved for the sake of the remark about first the Jews, then the Gentiles. "For that remark," Jesus says to the woman, "you may go home. The demon is driven out" (7, 29).

*　　*　　*

There are many such little stories in Mark, each complete in itself, each climaxing in some striking saying of Jesus. For example, just to continue with teaching on the Jew-Gentile problem and the replacement of the old order by the new, we have the five stories in 2, 1 to 3, 6. Each of these is an account of a clash between Jesus and the scribes and pharisees. In each one, the Jewish leaders make criticisms typical of the early Jewish attacks on the Christian communities, denying the right to forgive sins, to mingle and eat with the legally impure, the Gentile, the sinner; attacking their nonobservance of Jewish fasts, their neglect of the fine points of Sabbath observance, their general freedom in regard to the law, placing "doing good" above legal restrictions.

Each of the stories could stand alone as a brief illustration in a talk or as a sermon text. Here they are linked with one another and placed next to one another because of their similarity of content. Mark does not imply that the five events really happened in this order; if he meant that, he would hardly have omitted all indications of time. Nor, if this time question were important, would St. Matthew have split the stories up as he does, moving some of them to a place after the healing of Jairus' daughter and some even after the choice and sending of the apostles.

In each of the five stories Jesus confounds the adversaries with a powerful saying, and the first and last time by a healing as well: "The Son of Man has power on earth to forgive sins" (2, 10). "The sick have need of a physician, not the well. It is my mission to call sinners and not saints" (2, 17). "Can wedding guests fast while the bridegroom is with them?" (2, 19). "No one pours new wine into old wine skins" (2, 22). "The sabbath was made for man, not man for the sabbath. The Son of Man has authority over the sabbath" (2, 27). And after the fifth and last defeat, "The Pharisees walked out at once and consulted with the Herodians to plot against his life" (3, 6).

Now, still on the same general teaching theme, there is another group of stories at the end of Jesus' public life which parallels the group we have just looked at. Again there are five stories. Again the subject matter is controversy with the Jewish leaders. Again each story could stand alone (as some of them still do in the reading of the Sunday gospels). Each one centers on one point of attack from the Jewish parties and throws into prominence the words of Christ which apply to that problem and confute that adversary. The adversaries are, one after the other, representatives of each of the main groups struggling for power among the Jews: "The chief priests, the Scribes and the elders," "the Pharisees and the Herodians," "the Sadduccees," and "one of the Scribes."

This teaching unit, however, centers no longer on mere external observances, but on much deeper points of Christian-Jewish controversy: Jesus' authority (11, 27–33); God's rejection of Israel for their rejection of Christ (including also his divine sonship) (12, 1–12); the "render to Caesar" story (12, 13–17); the resurrection of the dead (12, 18–27); the great commandments of love (12, 28–34). And this series concludes, "From that time on, no one had the face to ask him any more questions" (12, 34).

Once again, notations of time and place are minimized. The controversies take place in Jerusalem and at the beginning of the first one is said: "As he walked about the temple grounds . . . " (11, 27). That is all we know. Attached to the five is a counterattack by Jesus: "And Jesus answered and said, teaching in the temple . . . " and Chapter 13 begins with the words, "As Jesus left the temple grounds . . . " and there follows the prophecy of the destruction of the temple and Jerusalem and of the whole old order which has rejected him, and the beginning of the days of the Son of Man (Christ and Church).

*   o   o

Let us turn to another major subject of instruction, the doctrine of the cross, the meaning of the "gospel" itself. Of course the whole passion story teaches this in act. But explicitly and in word, Mark sums it up in a long teaching section, 8, 27–10, 45. The section opens with the great identification scene on who Jesus really is. Then follows the "Son of Man" teaching. ("Son of Man" can include both Jesus and the community which follows him and is saved in him, just as the Son of Man in Daniel 7 is a single individual in the vision itself, but is afterward explained by the interpreting angel as the community of the elect.)

Now in this section Mark sums up the basic teaching on bearing the cross, submission, self-sacrifice, and dedication to the service of others after the model of Christ and as our way of salvation in him. The method Mark uses is very interesting. He shows how three times Christ foretells his own death and resurrection (8, 31–32; 9, 30–31; and 10, 32–34). Each time, immediately after reporting what Jesus said, the evangelist shows how the apostles had a false idea of what Christ's mission was about. The first time Jesus foretells the passion, Peter takes him aside and remonstrates with him. The second time, the apostles "could not see the drift of his remark and yet were too timid to ask him," and instead "discussed among themselves which one of their group was the greatest" (9, 32, 34). The third time, Jesus no sooner finishes speaking of his betrayal and condemnation, and of how he will be mocked and scourged and spit upon when James and John approach to ask, "Give us a seat, one at your right, the other at your left, in your glory" (10, 37).

And each of these three times, Jesus corrects their mistake by a fuller instruction on how they must follow him: 8, 34–38: they must bear the cross and freely part with their lives; 9, 33–37: who would be first must be servant of all and like a child; 10, 38–45: his followers must drink his chalice, undergo his baptism, be servant of all, as he himself was.

Into this same section are worked verses 43 to 48 of Chapter 9, on the absoluteness of the kingdom's demands: one must be ready to make any sacrifice for it; and verses 1 to 13 of Chapter 9, the transfiguration scene, in which Jesus is seen in glory. But on the way down the hill after the scene, the three apostles who have witnessed it discuss with him and one another "what 'resurrection from the dead' might really mean." Noteworthy for the same message is 10, 17-31, part of the same section, on giving up *all* for him and for the kingdom and for the gospel, as the rich young man will not do and as the apostles say they have already done. For this he promises them the reward of a hundred houses and mothers and children in this life — with persecutions — and in the world to come, life everlasting.

❋   ❋   ❋

But a gospel does not teach only with words, but also and especially with actions. A striking example of how it can do so is given by Mark immediately before and immediately after the important teaching section we have just looked at. This section outlined as fully as possible the real central gospel message, the suffering and glorified Christ as the object of their belief and their imitation. Now, before that section, they had not yet made a good beginning at understanding. Chapter 8, 14-21 is devoted to his reprimand to them, in which he even says their hearts are hardened (using the same words of them as he had used of the pharisees in 3, 5) and that having eyes they do not see, having ears they do not hear (as he had said of the crowds outside in 4, 12). Now he is going to begin the great teaching section to remedy that. And in 8, 22-26, just before the section begins, and just after his reproach to the disciples for failing to see, Mark relates how Christ cured a blind man, slowly, painfully, by stages, asking, "Do you see anything?" touching the man's eyes with spittle from his own mouth, and putting his hands on the man's eyes more than once until finally sight came.

But at the end of this section devoted to illuminating the apostles, Mark places another blind man's cure. This one comes eagerly to Jesus, crying for help, asks directly for what he needs and wants — "That I may see" — and Jesus says, "Your faith has saved you." And the man saw at once — and followed Jesus on his way (10, 46-52).

❋   ❋   ❋

A significant part of Mark's teaching with actions has to do with amplifying and explaining the gospel message that Christ is the fulfillment of the promises of the Old Testament. For instance, he begins his gospel with the Messianic quotation from Isaiah about the messenger who goes before the Lord. Then the description of John fulfills that quote. But there is more. John is described as Elijah in appearance, who was expected as forerunner of the Messiah.

John foretells one who will baptize with the Holy Spirit (cf. the prophecies of Ezekiel and of Joel in our Chapter 2). At Jesus' baptism, the Spirit does come upon him. Under its influence he moves into the desert, he begins preaching: the kingdom of God is close at hand. He calls the first disciples and begins to do the expected Messianic works: these are the healing signs and the preaching and the casting out of devils. In other words, the Messianic works are the conquering of all sorts of evil, moral and physical, the trampling underfoot of the whole kingdom of Satan.

And that is what Mark sets about showing Christ doing: from 1, 21 to 1, 45 healing sick and casting out demons are recorded alternately, and the people marvel. Sometimes the connection of sickness and demon is made explicit as in 9, 14–29, which speaks of the boy "possessed by a dumb spirit. Whenever he takes hold of the lad, he dashes him to the ground; and he foams and grinds his teeth and becomes rigid." Sometimes the connection with sin is made explicitly, as in the paralytic story, 2, 1–12; "Which is easier, to say to the paralytic, 'Your sins are forgiven you?' or to say, 'Rise, take up your mat and walk'?" And, in the face of criticisms Jesus does say, " 'Now I want you to understand that the Son of Man has power here on earth to forgive sins.' He then addressed the paralytic: '. . . Rise, take up your mat . . . and go home,' " which the man did (2, 10–11).

The same sin-sickness connection is evident in the saying: "The sick have need of a physician, not the healthy. It is my mission to call sinners and not saints" (2, 17). Or, as Jesus says to the paralytic in John's gospel: "Listen; you are now well and strong.

Do not sin any more or something worse will happen to you"
(Jn 5, 14).

In other miracles Mark stresses the fact that there is a mystery,
a hidden meaning, behind the miracle without telling us at the
moment exactly what that mystery is, as we saw for example after
the multiplications of loaves. Sometimes without saying anything
about the hidden meaning, the place he gives the miracle makes
his intention evident, as we saw of the blind men above.

Finally, there are other teachings in the miracles too, but these
are so obvious we hardly need to mention them here. The miracles
show the magnificence, power, and goodness of the person of
Christ. They show in case after case the need of approaching
him in faith, confidence, humility. They are often examples of
prayer, perseverance, gratitude. We repeat what we mentioned
in the past chapter: it is not by chance that preachers today find
so many of these virtues in the characters of the gospel story. The
stories designedly included such representative types of people
from the first. Finally, as was suggested in the past chapter, the
healings and exorcisms can and should be seen also as so many
exemplifications of the basic gospel message of death and resurrection itself. That is, they not only exemplify the traits of soul
with which one approaches Christ and the typical manner of
Christ's acting; they are, each of them, really the whole gospel
story exemplified in one individual human life. They show, every
one of them, how the turning to God through Christ out of one's
own helplessness, despair, and misery, with faith in him and in
his goodness, no matter how great the evil, and the patient
waiting for his cure and acceptance of his cure — how that really
is salvation.

◦   ◦   ◦

What about some of the "dogmatic" teachings we have mentioned as implied in the kerygma? The baptismal scene, for example, has another aspect beside Old Testament Messianic fulfillment. It is also a general teaching about the connection of
the Spirit with baptism. It must be read in the context of John
the Baptist's prediction that Jesus "will baptize you with the

Holy Spirit." The disciples will do the works Christ has done, when they have been baptized in the same Spirit as he. Even when they are sent out on their first mission (6, 7–13) "they exhorted the people to a change of heart; they also drove out many demons and cured many persons." The fullness of this comes in the final sending at the end of the gospel.

Mark also teaches that baptism is connected with sacrificial self-offering. At Jesus' baptism, the voice from heaven had said, "You are my beloved Son, in you I am well pleased." There is an intentional reference here to the figure of the servant in Isaiah, a figure whose destiny is related in Isaiah 53, to suffer for the sins of the people. The beloved son is also Isaac, who, in Jewish contemporary tradition, had willingly accepted the role of sacrificial victim, according to God's command to his father Abraham.

✿   ✿   ✿

Christ's divine sonship, to take another example, is implied in the baptism passage, in the voice at the transfiguration, and in at least two of the parables. But it is especially taught not in any one passage so much as in the development of the whole gospel, as we shall see in the next section on Mark's general outline. The same must be said for the important doctrinal point of the Church: in Mark, rather than explained or taught in any one word or short story, the Church is a theme and an aspect of the whole gospel, perhaps the aspect which Mark wished above all others to stress and communicate, the key to his theology.

Liturgical influence we have already seen in the account of the multiplication of the loaves, modeled on the Christian Eucharist. But the same influence appears in the account of the Last Supper itself. This account is almost certainly a recording of the actual words used in the Christian Eucharist, just like the excerpt from the same liturgy which Paul preserves for us in 1 Corinthians, 11, 23–26. If the gospel account is the recording of a liturgical formula, we can understand how the words over the bread and wine, for instance, come to be reported differently in the different gospels.

Substantially of course all four accounts we have are in agreement; they differ only in details. But we can hardly explain the differences in detail simply by saying that the evangelists, as historians, did not consider this point in their history important enough to be reproduced exactly. We can hardly suppose that although they intended to write word for word what our Lord spoke that night, they did not take the trouble to ask the apostles diligently exactly what it was he had said. Even the explanation that Mark's slight difference from Matthew is to be attributed to a desire for brevity does not really explain. Why should he be concerned for brevity, here of all places? Mark tells the story of the storm at sea in 121 words as against Matthew's 72; he describes the first multiplication of loaves in 144 words where Matthew does it in 120. Why at this high point in our Lord's life should Mark shorten, even by two or three words, a sentence which Christ has asked his followers explicitly to repeat to the end of time in memory of him?

On the other hand, the differences are understandable if what the gospels are recording literally and word for word is the account of the Last Supper which was passed on in the Christian liturgy. That account could differ slightly from place to place by the time the gospels were written, just as the liturgical form of the words of consecration used today in the canon of our Roman rite mass differs from the form used in the Armenian rite and neither of them agrees in all details with any one of the four forms preserved in the New Testament.

ROMAN LITURGY: "For this is the cup of my blood of the new and eternal covenant, the mystery of faith, which shall be poured out for you and for many unto the remission of sins. As often as you shall do this, you shall do it in memory of me."

ARMENIAN LITURGY: "This is my blood of the new covenant, which is poured out for you and for many unto expiation and forgiveness of sin."

1 CORINTHIANS (11, 25): "This cup is the new covenant in my blood. Do this as often as you drink it, in remembrance of me."

MATTHEW (26, 28): "For this is my blood of the covenant

which is poured out for many for the forgiveness of sins."

MARK (14, 24): "This is my blood of the covenant which is poured out for many."

LUKE (22, 20): "This cup is the new covenant in my blood, which is poured out for you."

❖   ❖   ❖

There is another level of interpretation which many have turned to recently in their attempts to work out the evangelist's intended theology. This level takes into account the fact that the eastern literature of that time rejoiced in symbolism and in hidden parabolic effects. Thus some notice that the words "sleep" and "rise" are used of Jairus' daughter (5, 21–43) exactly as St. Paul uses them of the Christian dead. And Jesus speaks to the girl and takes her by the hand and raises her up, as, in the early preaching, God raised him up, and as all who are in the graves will hear his voice and he will raise them up and will give them eternal life. In other words, the simple story of how Jesus brought this dead girl back to life is told in such a way as to include a good deal of Christian teaching about the resurrection of the dead in general. And thus when the bystanders laugh Jesus to scorn for saying she is only sleeping, they are simply taking the position which nonbelievers regularly took in regard to the believing Christians, even such learned nonbelievers as the Greeks of the Areopagus who turned aside from a lecture on this subject by St. Paul (Acts 17, 16–34).

❖   ❖   ❖

Some ask whether the story of the anointing at Bethany (14, 3–9) is not somehow modeled after a liturgical anointing — the same anointing mentioned in regard to the apostles in 6, 13, and probably that of James 5, 3–15, which the Council of Trent points out is connected with our Sacrament of Anointing.

❖   ❖   ❖

It has been noticed how often and even regularly phrases like "Does anything hinder?" or "What hinders?" or "Since there is no hindrance" appear in New Testament accounts of baptism. It has been asked if there is not then a hidden meaning in the story of the little children who came to Jesus for a blessing and were turned away by the apostles (10, 13–16). "Let the little children come to me," Jesus replies, "and *do not hinder them*, for of such is the kingdom of heaven." Strengthening the probable connection with baptism is the resemblance: "Unless one receive the kingdom of God as a little child, he shall not enter into it" and "Unless a man be baptized with water and the Holy Spirit, he cannot enter the kingdom of heaven" (Jn 3, 5).

* * *

An investigation has been made into possible symbolism in the vocabulary with which Christ's burial is recounted. When Joseph of Arimathea, who is "looking for the kingdom of God," goes down with the body of Jesus into a rock-hewn tomb ("The Rock was Christ") — and takes with him new cloths and ointments, is all this related somehow to baptismal ceremonies in the Church and to the thought that "in baptism you are buried together with him unto death that with Christ you may rise to newness of life" (Col 2, 12)?

* * *

Many of these recent studies perhaps strike us as strange. They are only lines of investigation, along which scholars are trying to penetrate to the real theological message of Mark's gospel, presented as that message is entirely in terms of what happened to Christ during his lifetime. Unfortunately we cannot go on to give any adequate picture of all the work that is being done. The material is simply too abundant and too many-sided. For further examples the reader is recommended to turn to scholarly journals like the *Catholic Biblical Quarterly, Scripture,* or — for occasional New Testament articles — to issues of *Theological Studies* in recent years, as well as the pages of *The Bible Today* for more popular presentations.

* * *

The third element in the composition of a gospel is the individual plan or theology of the whole: something beyond the message itself, or rather a certain aspect of the message, which Mark wishes particularly to stress. Here too the problem is the extraordinary richness of the material, which consequently lends itself to interpretation along several different lines. Nevertheless, all suggested outlines agree in certain points, listed in the Introductions as "the theology" or the "theological outlook" or "doctrinal interests" of Mark. They include then — this much is obvious — such facts as a certain community of ideas with St. Paul, a certain stressing of universalism, of the fact that the gospel is for the entire world, pagans as well as Jews; a special interest in the mystery of the Person of Jesus — Jesus as the Son of Man, Jesus as the Son of God. All notice Mark's concern to make his story intelligible to the non-Jewish audience of Rome for which he wrote. Most admit his special interest in St. Peter and frequent reflection of Peter's point of view, in accord with the tradition that Mark's gospel sums up and represents Peter's teaching.

But when it comes to an actual outline, there is, as with the other gospels too, considerable diversity as to details. We shall present four typical constructions that the reader may judge for himself and at least see how theological interpretation today tends to proceed.

1. Some see Mark's theme in the gradual revelation of the identity of Jesus. Up to 8, 27, Jesus is gradually making understood that he is the Messiah. From then on, the stress is on the fact that he is the Son of Man with the mission of suffering to fulfill.

A variation of this notes a gradually increasing revelation centered really around the idea "Son of God." Mark opens with the words, "The gospel of Jesus Christ, the Son of God." A voice from heaven says, "You are my Son." The demons recognize Jesus as "the Son of God," but he orders them to be silent. He cures a paralytic to prove his ability to do what the Pharisees have just said only God can do — forgive sins. He impresses the people and his disciples with his authority and power. He brings to a head the ever mounting interest in his real identity at 8, 27 with the question to the apostles, "Who do you say that I am?"

He makes it clearer to them that he is someone for whom they must be willing to lay down their lives, someone who will come in the glory of God to judge the world. At the Transfiguration a voice from heaven identifies him for the apostles: "This is my beloved Son." His own final parables show that he is the Son of the divine Master of the vineyard and that he is David's Lord. And finally, on trial for his life, he states the full truth openly before the world: "Are you the Christ, the Son of the Ever Blessed?" "I am." — And they condemn him for blasphemy. When he is dead, the pagan soldier standing guard at his cross says, "Indeed this man was the Son of God."

Historians and philologists can point out how susceptible of other meanings the words "son of God" were in Judaism and how unlikely it is that a pagan soldier could have meant "truly-begotten Son of the one true God." These things are true. But the pattern in what Mark wrote is too strongly marked to be merely accidental. Mark, who taught along with Peter and Paul, believed in Jesus as the Son of God, and he builds a gospel around the eternally challenging question, "Who is this Man?" and "What think you of Christ? Whose Son is he?"

2. Others point out an outline in Mark built around the idea that what happens to Christ must happen to his followers — to the individual and to the group, the Church. Jesus calls disciples, saying "Follow me!" He chooses twelve among them; they become his real family, in contrast to his physical relatives. To them he interprets the meaning of the parables. They live with him and experience his power over fever, leprosy, sin, the Law, demons, and death; they share his rejections too.

He sends them out to preach and cure and cast out demons as he himself was doing. At the time of their sending, the story of the martyrdom of John the Baptist is told — casting a shadow over their future and his. They return to him, but with him and like him they can have no rest from salvific work. They feed the five thousand who come to him in the desert, arranging the people in orderly groups, passing out the food he has blessed, and gathering up the fragments afterward. They learn only gradually what this means. They bring the sick to him from all the country around. He defends them again and again against the pharisees, and he teaches them what true cleanliness and true observance of the Law must be. They are his ministers once again in the feeding of the four thousand, symbolically directed to the pagan world, but afterward they still do not understand. They are preaching in his name, but they do not yet hear his real message, so they cannot speak plainly — like the deaf man who "spoke only imperfectly" and whom Jesus cured slowly and with effort in 7, 31–36. They do not understand, they have eyes and do not see, in spite of his teaching thus far — like the blind man whom Christ cures in laborious stages in 8, 22–26. So in 8, 27 Jesus begins his series of direct instructions to them on the heart of his message. Three times he foretells his passion and resurrection and follows the predictions with lessons which bring out the fact that his followers will have to share these things with him. After the instructions, they can be represented by a blind man who sees at once at Jesus' word, whose faith has saved him, and who rises up "and follows Jesus on his way." Nevertheless, in the actual crisis of the passion, they fail and abandon Jesus, but his first word after he rises is a message for them. And in the final summary at the end of the gospel, he sends them forth to preach his word in all the world, and assists them from heaven in all they do.

3. A third possible approach to the outline of Mark is based on the divisions found marked in the text in the oldest manuscripts of the gospel. These indicate that Mark might have been composed for reading in small segments throughout the liturgical year. There are enough such segments, taking one for each Sunday, to read the gospel down to the beginning of the final ministry in Jerusalem (11, 1). Taking it that way, one finds the gospel down to this point is divided into four major parts, which correspond to the four seasons of the Jewish liturgical year, beginning with the New Year after Tabernacles in September (1, 1–3, 6; 3, 7–6, 6; 6, 7–8, 26; 8, 27–10, 45). Similarities of development within each of these four parts and certain correspondences with

the feasts of the year as they occur lend weight to this opinion. The following section, the Jerusalem ministry, would have constituted special reading matter for the days of the solemn feast of Tabernacles, and the passion-resurrection story would have been reading for the days of the paschal ceremonies.

4. A fourth modern approach notes the apparently interlocking cycles of events in Mark, so that the instructions and healings of the first part all seem to foreshadow, in order and type, the lessons and great events of the last part. The raising of Jairus' daughter, the rejection at Nazareth, and the sending of the apostles, for example, would have been deliberately placed as they are by Mark to parallel the resurrection of Jesus, the rejection of Jesus by his people, and the post-resurrection sending and Pentecost. Again, the movement from the synagogue to the house of the disciples in the first chapter would deliberately recall the order of salvation and preaching — the house of the disciples being also (as normally in the first generation) the gathering place of the community, the church. There seem to be other such alternating patterns discernible: revelation of teaching is followed regularly by separate explanation to the disciples, healings alternate with exorcisms, etc.

o   o   o

A few words on the other gospels:

All four gospels maintain of course the basic kerygmatic outline, for a gospel must above all "preach the gospel." Matthew and Luke follow Mark fairly closely, but they work in much more of explicit teaching material. They present many more sayings of Jesus, and even weave together scattered individual sayings to make whole sermons which do not appear in Mark. Matthew and Luke also make more explicit much of Mark's symbolism as well as many of his Old Testament allusions. They do some rearranging of events to fit their own overall presentation. Matthew, for example, puts so much emphasis on Christ's verbal teaching that he seems to make all the rest, the actions and stories, revolve around the five or six long discourses which stand out so prominently in his gospel. Most striking perhaps in Luke is the drive toward Jerusalem; so that ten chapters of his gospel are devoted to Jesus' steady forward movement in the direction of his final destiny in the holy city.

John selects a very few striking miracles which sum up the general lines of all Christ's works of healing and of divine power, and he presents them in such a way that their strong charge of theological significance cannot be missed. Often he underlines his theological intention by attaching to Jesus' action an explicit commentary on the theological significance of what is done, as notably in Chapter 6 on the true bread, Chapter 9 on the blind seeing, or Chapter 11 on the resurrection of the dead.

John also singles out a few terms capable of bearing heavy theological significance, and then uses these as themes and motifs in the development of his gospel. That is, he introduces these words early in his gospel, and then has them reappear again and again, weaving their way artistically through the whole: terms like life, light, truth, Son and sons, witness, judgment, etc. The same terms appear in John's epistles.

So marked are traits like these in John that he has been recognized in almost every age as a theologian par excellence. He has even been accused by some of not having written a gospel like the other gospels at all, but rather a pure theological treatise with a few made-up examples to illustrate his doctrinal points. Now one sees rather that his gospel is a gospel like the others, with the same basic message to convey about the great thing God has really done for us in Christ. And it has the same secondary aim of explaining that message through the words and actions of Jesus, just as the apostolic Church did in all her teaching and preaching. The main difference between John and the others is that John, using a more obviously stylized approach and making his reflections and applications and illusions more explicit than had the others, makes his theological purpose more evident than they had theirs.

Not however that John can be called obvious. Far from it. To begin with, the general nature of middle eastern art and literature would make that most unlikely even apriori. But in actual fact too, the more John has been studied in recent years the clearer it has become how profound and how subtle he is — not only as a theologian, but also as a writer and as an artist. For instance, the appealing and attractive symbols of the first half of his gospel — bread, wine, fruit, life, living water, light, etc. — turn out in the second half of the gospel (Chapter 13 and following) to have been veiled passion-teaching. They stand for faith in Jesus; they stand for faith in his word, which is God's word, which is a message of death and resurrection and the triumphing over death through faith and love; which is — incarnate — Jesus himself. Jesus' long discourse at the Last Supper (as also the Joannine epistles) bring out these meanings on a verbal level, and the passion and resurrection, as in the other gospels, bring out these meanings most compellingly and definitively of all — in act.

❊   ❊   ❊

After stressing so much the doctrinal material in the four gospels, is it perhaps necessary to remind ourselves again of the gospels' other, more obvious side? Of how the gospels are truly and by the deliberate intention of their authors also por-traits of Christ? They draw a consistent picture of the most extraordinary personality the world has ever known. That it is a living picture, a plausible picture, an appealing picture needs no demonstration here. All those who have known and read the gospels can testify to that. That it is an historical picture is ulti-mately the only possible explanation of the life that breathes in it, of its internal consistency, and of its transcendental quality — the fact that it is simply beyond the creative power of human literary imagination, just as it has proved through the centuries to be beyond the power of human literary imitation.

The examples we have seen must not then leave us with the impression that the gospels were concatenations of conundrums under the superficial guise of a life of Christ. For we must re-member that according to the very theological intentions of the authors such a fake gospel would have made no sense. For the Christian theology they wanted to present was not a matter of abstract theses and propositions, which could then be illustrated by little stories and examples. The Christian theology they were presenting, the same one we have studied in earlier chapters on the apostolic preaching, was a theology which depended completely on the reality of that one life. It was a theology which grew entirely out of faith in a real Person, and faith that something had really happened to him, and faith that that something was God's message for the redemption of all mankind.

The gospels are explaining that message, they are describing that happening, and they are presenting that Person. The best and perhaps the only fully convincing argument that they intended to present him as real and living, as he actually was and as they had known him, is ultimately to pick up the gospels and read them and meet him there ourselves.

❊   ❊   ❊

THE WORD IN THE BODY OF CHRIST

CHAPTER 15

Down Through the Ages

THE good news itself, with the most important conclusions to be drawn from it and the most important dispositions necessary to receive it, was then, under the inspiration of the Spirit, summed up in the written gospels, and thus summed up in Christ. Historically, this was a summing up of the Christianity of the first and second Christian generations; but by God's special providence and direction, using the authors of the gospels and the events they recorded as his instruments to produce the picture he wanted, it was also a summing up of the essentials about the message for all generations to come. "Jesus Christ is the same yesterday, today, and forever" (Heb 13, 8).

Still, a message, to be really a message, has to be conveyed from one mind to another. God, God's mind, does not change. And the word of the Lord abides forever. But men and the minds of men do change constantly. If then the message is to be effective as a message, and if it is to remain really the same and continue to have the same effect in those who come afterward as it had in those who came before, the message must be constantly preached and explained in ever new terms, terms constantly adapted to the changed and changing audience. Only new and different terms will mean to the new audience what the old terms meant to the old.

On the most obvious level of course this is the reason for translation from one language to another. The first Christians heard the word in Hebrew, Aramaic, or Greek. Few people do nowadays. And passing the gospel on to the changed men of today in Hebrew, Aramaic, and Greek would not produce the effect desired. If the message, as message, as contact between the mind of God and the minds and hearts of men, is to remain the same, the expression of the message in words must change.

But a little reflection shows that this principle has much more than merely linguistic implications. Not only languages change, but customs and attitudes and interests and knowledge and presuppositions. Whole cultures come and go. They have done so from the beginning of human life on this planet and they continue to do so today. And for all we know, a hundred million years from now, on a myriad of planets today still undiscovered, the infinite resources of human ingenuity, and folly, may continue to produce new human ways and standards of thought and action along lines still beyond our wildest dreams.

But the word of God abides forever. And in its written form, the word of God is fixed in the Bible. If mustard seeds and publicans and the phenomena of demonic possession have to be explained to people today before they get the full force of a gospel story, what may it be in the future? In a society that no longer knew the meaning of kings and kingdoms, masters and slaves, stewards and householders, money and taxes? Among a conceivable postatomic race of burrowers underground, who no longer knew the meaning of sun and light and wind or the sowing of seed or the sprouting of grain?

The gospel message of salvation will remain the same. It is aimed at the deepest places in man's heart which cannot change unless a man escape from his eternally inquiring intellect and infinitely hungering will, or unless he shake off his own finiteness and truly become God. In no matter what far-off world of the future, if there is a future, there will be no other name under heaven given to men in which they must be saved. And yet, if the message is to continue to ring true in all the changing circumstances under which men will have to hear it, the simple reading of the New Testament alone will not suffice.

That is another important reason for the existence of the Church.

The fact that God has given us his message in a fixed verbal form implies the necessity of a living Church in which that message will be adequately presented to all succeeding ages. The Church has been performing that function now these two thousand years. She takes the foundation God has given her in the message as preached by the apostles to men of the first century; gives it in its inspired, written form, a place of priority in all her teaching and preaching; and in generation after generation, age after age, and on many different cultural levels within any one age, she brings that message to life. This is the process we want to examine briefly in this chapter.

*　　*　　*

God, as Author of scripture, saw to it that a first pattern for this process of adapting the message to different hearers and moving from one culture to another should be incorporated into the New Testament itself. The disputes about the right to preach to the Gentiles and about the observances to be imposed on pagan converts mark the biggest cultural transition the Church has ever had to go through — the passage from Judaism to Christianity. And the process as we see it in that first changeover lays down certain laws for similar changes down through the ages: the change comes about first by external, seemingly "accidental" circumstances; it regards in the first place material, external observances; it forces a rethinking of the meaning of the whole past in the light of the message itself; it gives birth to a future which looks different on the outside but is only the more truly the same — which possesses more securely all it really possessed and treasured before, but is unencumbered by accidentals which, it sees now, were never really part of God's message, but only aids to presenting the message to men of a particular time and place.

The New Testament itself also sets a model for the Church's wrestlings with heresy and schism, another providential means down through the ages to force the Church to greater perfection in her understanding of the message. And the New Testament shows us Church order and Church law growing up to fill the keenly felt gaps as the Church moves more and more into regular contact with godless pagan society.

We noticed in Chapter 11 how the New Testament community lashed back at heresy above all insofar as heresy was an attack on the message itself and insofar as corruptions in doctrine led necessarily to an inability to live out in its fullness that Christian life which spontaneously flows from the real message. The Church has never lost this point of view. Her concern in repelling heresy down through the ages has been centered on the necessity of saving men, and keeping pure the deposit of truth which she possesses that that truth may remain a path on which men mount to God. Deviations from this salvific truth, even when they are completely new deviations, using words, raising problems which have never appeared before, she feels at once as deviations, and rejects. It is not the new formulae of words that disturb her; she has experience enough of the wide variety of ways in which one truth can be expressed. It is not the raising of new problems that frightens her; having repelled a false answer she never rests content until a true and satisfactory answer to the new problem has been found.

Again when she does decide that this or that answer is false she does not always do so in terms of some contrary formulation which she explicitly, consciously possesses. For instance, we saw earlier, it does not seem that any explicit, positive teaching of the "consubstantiality" of the divine Persons was in the Church long before Nicea. And many of the early fathers could and did write at least vaguely erroneous statements on the subject. But when Arius once put into words the "There was a time when he was not" in regard to Christ, the Church recognized at once that a blow was being struck at the heart of the good news. Arius might not have been conscious of it, probably was not in fact. But the Church was, and she condemned it.

So too with the Docetist errors. Those who taught them may have thought they were teaching a more worthy doctrine. Perhaps they even said: "It would have been more fitting for God to have saved us without actually taking a human body or without actually dying on the cross. And God could have saved us this way. Therefore he did." Arguments to the contrary, based on the evident facts of Christ's human nature, appeals to what had been seen and touched, could all be refuted as mere proofs of the excellence of the "appearance" God had put on.

But the Church saw Docetism as vitiating the good news, tearing something out of the very heart of it. Jesus, without a real human nature, a real body in which he really accepted suffering and death, would no longer be good news to us. If the resurrection did not really happen to a real man, there is no good news at all.

It may be true that what happened to Christ was a sign and symbol of what does and will happen to us who follow him, but it is a case of reality symbolizing reality. If what happened to Christ were *only* a symbol, not something that really happened, if it were only a fiction symbolizing reality, then it might all be true as true can be *as a symbol* — but it would not be a basis for faith and hope and love. But the Church knows that faith and hope and love are exactly what men need to make them able to share in and reap the benefits of God's offered salvation. She instinctively rejects all forms of Docetism. Monophysite and Nestorian errors would have to be rejected for similar reasons. The salvation had to be *real*, it had to be *ultimate*, leaving nothing further to be demanded or desired; it had to be an act of divine love and self-giving. If Christ is not really God or not really man or is some third thing between the two, these salvific truths cannot be verified in him.

Pelagius would have men reach perfection on their own efforts, simply by following the example Jesus had given. It was a keen understanding of one part of the message, but it was to miss another equally important part. Christ came to save us from our sins, and this salvation came not from our own power but from the Holy Spirit of God. Implied in the message of salvation is man's helplessness without God, man's inability to live up to all that a man should be. And the message too is a message of divine love for man — God had not, then, put man into this wretched state, man had chosen it for himself — every man, beginning with the very first one who ever existed.

Besides, they knew this from the Old Testament: man freely rejected God's plan for him. Had man lived without sin, had no one ever lied, cheated, stolen, disobeyed, failed to love, then the world today could be a paradise. But man, from his first creation, has rejected this plan of God's. The sin of the first man introduced sin into the world and with it the whole pattern of death and destruction, misery and failure apart from God, which has marked the entire history of mankind.

This is the picture of man without God, sinful, twisted, lost. And the good news is that God stoops to man, who has chosen and still chooses daily that wretched state. God stoops to him, comes to him, and offers him a return to the original plan of love and peace. What a gift! How to get it? By believing that this unjust death on the cross, like all injustices and all inexplicable horrors of human life, is the result of sin, of lovelessness and God-lessness; by admitting, in this belief, that sin tends naturally to such results, and that I have sinned; by accepting such results in my life therefore, if they occur and when, as deserved; but also as God's gift, in the belief that through them, accepted as and with and in Christ, I too can reach the transformation of the resurrection he attained by his love and obedience. And so one enters on a new life of faith and hope and love.

Knock out original sin from this picture, the dogma that God's original plan for man was a life in perfect love with the natural results therefrom of peace and joy; the dogma that man, beginning with the very first man, rejected this divine plan; the dogma that the rejection of the very first man, the first introduction of sin into the world, has influenced all his descendants, parents passing on to their children, generation after sinful generation, legacies of sin in bad habits, unjust social orders, weakened, crippled, diseased bodies, etc., and above all the fact that children are not born into an order where grace, divine life, love, and the influence of the supernatural reign over all — knock out all this, and the doctrine of good news crumbles into dust.

This list could be continued indefinitely. To take some of the more difficult examples:

The sixteenth-century Reformers emphasized one aspect of the message — God's pure gift — to the neglect of others — man's participation, for example, and the sacramental principle. More seriously, they proved unable to accept with all its consequences the fact that salvation is a group affair, in one group, one visible Body of Christ, organized and structured by one Spirit through visible teachers and rulers.

In more recent times, the definition of the infallibility of the Pope seems above all aimed at saving that practical unity of the one Body. The Church is so united in love and obedience that when her visible head speaks out in the fullness of his role as visible head, she rightly sees him as endowed "with that infallibility with which Christ wished that his Church should be endowed" (First Council of the Vatican, DB 1839).

The modern Marian definitions are an exemplification in one human person of the fullness of the message. In defining the Assumption, the Church proclaims that the one who has yielded herself completely to God according to the full and perfect pattern of the gospel, receives the highest and fullest reward. What happens to her is a model instance of what participation in Christ can mean and of how it can elevate a simple human being.

In the definition of the Immaculate Conception, stress is laid on the fact that even the heights of perfect participation in Christ are more the work of God than of man. Mary received her grace and the Spirit of love and obedience as God's free gift from the first instant of her existence, and it is on the basis of that gift that she rose to the heights a human being can reach. "To him who has shall be given."

Dogmas are the Church's instinctive and infallible reaction to attempts to rob her of part of the gospel or to make the gospel less truly "good news," less proclaimable, preachable, less of a joy to the world. Such false movements or false interpretations of a part of the message bump harshly against all that she already knows and does and is. She reacts and rejects, and in doing so she refines, teaches, proclaims, makes explicit.

But even after having attained a fixed formulation of such truths, the Church still puts them to different uses at different times. Thus she presents scholastic answers in an age which raises scholastic questions, legal when the scientific questions and answers and predominant thought patterns of an age are legal. She can be firm with the barbarians, subtle with the Greeks. Nineteenth-century cries that the gospels are myth or fable or valueless hearsay accounts will be met with a firm insistence that they are not myth, not fable, not hearsay; they are history. But when twentieth-century openness to the value of symbolism and adult appreciation for the diversity of literary forms makes it possible, she stresses theoretically too what she always had practically: that the gospels are theology in the flesh.

*   *   *

But so far we have been speaking of the Church's formal teaching, her presentation and defense of the message in speaking and writing, in formula and word. But there is still another whole side to her teaching. She forms little children in Christ in thousands of different ways, and in practice most people reach and hear the message in the Church without ever knowing much about the theoretical defense of the message, even as against the most burning scientific difficulties or heretical objections of their own day. The teaching, as clear and scientifically exact as possible, must be there in the Church some place. It must be available for those who need it, and they are many. It sheds its light on all the other levels of life in the Church in different ways. But still most people attain the message and the salvation it promises without knowing too much personally about these theoretical formulations.

How do they do it? They do it by living in the Church. For the Church is the living gospel and the gospel is Christ. Whoever tries to be a part of her will find himself in contact, living contact, with the essential Christian message. For us then to grasp the Church as the living continuation of the word of the gospel down through the ages would require more than simply examining what the Church has officially or even unofficially taught in word. We cannot grasp her or the fullness of her teaching on the level of words and propositions alone. She teaches and forms with all she is. The theologian would have to grasp, to understand her in all her living reality, insofar as this is possible, if he really wants to be able to express scientifically all the Church is "teaching" at any given moment.

The Church exists for all men of all times and in all places. That means today, for instance, as well for Australian bushmen, Central European peasants, and Chinese mandarins, as for the couple who run the tavern at the corner and the doctor they visit, the professor who buys lunch there, the monk in the mountain retreat. They all belong to the one Church. And she belongs to all of them. The child and the sage, the idiot, the genius, the weak and the strong, the sinner and the saint, the man and the woman, the black and the white. Each of them has at every moment a full right to the whole Christian message.

Now this is a very complex operation and it has been so from the beginning. St. Paul's "all things to all men that I may gain them all" was not just rhetoric. Nor was it merely wily dealing. It was a reality, and is one today. The Church's message must reach all men at all levels; to this end it must be — and always has been — expressed in a wide variety of ways.

There are people whom practically no formula of words could ever really touch, but who can hear and receive the good news in the sight of a crucifix, some again in the sight of a splendid church building, others in the loving service of a dedicated priest or nun, others . . . but the list could go on forever. Raised as Catholics but without much instruction, or converted perhaps by technically "inadequate" motives — they see nevertheless that the finger of God is here.

Ask of any of these an account in words of what he has received, of what the story of his salvation is, and the accounts may differ widely; in fact, some may have no account to offer. But all will recite and accept, according to their ability to understand, the one creed.

It is really important to stress how great this diversity can be. English stories about Irish maids sometimes paint a picture of a purgatory-and-indulgences obsessed sort of mind, relieved only by an occasional reference to rosaries, novenas, confession boxes, and "contribute to the support of our pastors." Non-Catholic missionaries tell of backward South American villages where the people know only their saints and their shrines and a few feast days, but seem to have no knowledge of the gospel.

And yet in both of these, and in hundreds of other sorts of cases, variations on one theme, many a pastor who has worked with these people in practice insists on the deep Christian faith and the high Christian sanctity people sometimes actually attain by these "inadequate" means. What is the explanation? The explanation is life in the living Church, which presents — not always even deliberately and consciously — the one message to different people in different ways.

Here is another frequent error of reformers of all times. They see, for example, that this point or that belongs to the gospel, a certain understanding, about life, reality, God. And they insist that it be preached and accepted and practiced *formally*. It can be by some. But not by all. So those some join the sect. But they cannot succeed in producing a Catholic Church. The simplest and clearest example of this is perhaps the sixteenth-century Reformation insistence on reading the Bible. Of course reading the Bible is good and necessary where possible. But it is not, as a matter of fact, possible for all. Not now anyway. Perhaps some day, but not now. And certainly not in the sixteenth century. So their reform could appeal to some, but not to all.

Similarly, the Church of the gospels is a Church of saints, and all Christians should be without sin. But as a simple matter of fact, not all men have yet grown up to that level of the gospel, perhaps they never will. But the Church of Jesus Christ must be for all. And so some form sects of saints, but these sects break off from the body of Christians and become heresies. The true reformers, the real saints, who understand what the Church is and what the gospels are really saying, form voluntary associations within the Church to make life according to the highest ideals possible to those capable of seeing and understanding and consequently desiring it. Such are, for instance, the religious orders, the secular institutes, lay apostolate movements, charitable organizations, etc. But even these, with all the thousands of good Christians in and outside of them, are, in the long run, only a part of the Church. The whole Church includes the weak, the falling, and the fallen; all, however, pointing and pointed toward the one great ideal in the one living body.

And this finally leads to showing the absurdity of judging the Church as she is in terms of only a part of herself; of saying for instance that she has included persecutors, tyrants, totalitarian rulers, when the gospels preach love, service, humility. Of course this is true. But through the centuries and according to the limiting and limited abilities of the poor sinful men who are her members, she with the grace of God always points beyond, leads forward. And in every generation she produces in abundance those who do succeed completely, and only these does she recognize as her saints.

The Church is at every moment and in every place far richer than what can be put into the words of a description. She lives. And he who would know her, and theologize about her must live with her. Doing so, he finds in all this diversity a wonderful consistency and unity. To each according to his fashion and to each according to his ability and needs, the Church is bringing the good news, God's Word Incarnate. That is what she is.

POSTSCRIPT

Postscript on Biblical Theology

THEOLOGY is, in the first and primary sense, an understanding of the faith, *intellectus fidei*. But there is only one faith. Therefore, in the full sense of the word, implying a perfect understanding, there can be only one theology.

Still, among men, the likelihood of anyone's ever attaining that absolutely perfect understanding which can take in the whole object of the faith comprehensively and perfectly is absolutely nil. Our understanding is limited, in its individual acts, in its objects, and in the actual sum total of its acts and objects at and up to any one moment. And so no one achieves this one perfect understanding of faith, this one final theology in which everything has been seen. Such a theology is a goal that we work at, each individual theologian throughout his one short lifetime, and the whole corps of the Church's theologians throughout any one generation, and the whole long line of theologians down through the ages.

The perfect theology remains always only a goal at which we aim, toward which we work. If it ever were to be attained, it would be one and single. But because of our imperfection, our obtuseness, and our positive errors, theology, in this first sense of an understanding which can exist in any one mind or group of minds, continues multiple. We pick away at it. The truths, the insights, which would make it up are there, being presented to us at every moment in the Church. But we grasp them one day, see them perhaps a little more fully the next, forget some part of them on a third day, and so on through a theological lifetime.

Still, because the minds God has given us are insatiable appetites for truth, we go on trying.

In a second sense, derived from the first, theology is the expression of what we have understood in words, in a system, in a school. Here again, because of human imperfection and the necessity of proceeding by way of only partial insights, there is and there has always been abundant room for multiplicity. Different systems and schools, different formal approaches to theology, to the perfect expression of what understanding we have gained, are formed, grow and expand, show themselves fertile, unite perhaps with others, sometimes die.

Human imperfection and inability to express (or even to investigate) fully all reality at once is also a cause for multiplicity. As a necessary consequence, there spring up theologies of different materials, so many different starting places for investigation. Thus, for example, there exist traditionally such branches as dogmatic theology, moral theology, ascetical and mystical theology; courses are offered in Oriental, in liturgical, in pastoral theology, etc. Ideally — an ideal which remains unattainable — these all form but one perfect structure rising out of one perfect insight into the depths of all the supernatural truth God has proposed to us, with all its implications for Christian living and with all its presuppositions in the world of things as they are.

Biblical theology as ordinarily understood and practiced today falls within this last group, theologies of different materials. It is a theology, an attempt to understand the faith, with a specialized starting place, with a special, limited material for investigation. Biblical theology is, in this sense, the theology of the Bible, the attempt to understand the faith as it is presented to us in the pages of the Bible. New Testament theology would be a subdivision of that.

New Testament theology, like all theology, grows through various stages, progressing step by step. As a first step, it must determine what the New Testament is saying. This is exegesis. What is the meaning of the texts? What is this New Testament author or that one trying to say? This too has its presuppositions and preparations, and they are long and hard. Exegesis, while only the first step in biblical theology, is already itself the end of a long and dusty road. To arrive at a definitive interpretation, understanding, exegesis of any one block of text is no small achievement. And no matter how well it is once achieved, later and further research seems to be always opening new doors, so that it is a rare book of the New Testament which can survive more than a decade without some new commentary appearing and trying to get out of the familiar biblical page still more of the meaning or a still more exact expression of the meaning which that book had for its human author when he wrote it.

Still, in biblical theology, all this is only the first step. The second step is the attempt to reconstruct the "theologies" of individual writers and groups of writers within the New Testament. In this step occur works on "the theology of St. Paul," "the theology of the Joannine writings," etc. Here the investigator attempts to build up a comprehensive picture of the God-centered world view from which this or that writer worked. Proceeding from an exact exegesis, one tries to see and express as one whole the general outline that was in the author's mind in all its theological richness. As much as possible one here confines himself to using the very expressions of the inspired author himself. One tries to give the whole summary picture of the Pauline doctrine of the Church as the Body of Christ, for example, gathering fragments from various Pauline letters, carefully studied and compared. And then one tries to see how this Body of Christ on earth fitted into Paul's general view of God, Christ, man, of the redemption, of the Christian life, etc. From all this, one attempts to construct a Pauline synthesis which remains, if and when perfectly achieved, something expressed from beginning to end in Pauline categories and Pauline language. To stay with our example of the Church, one does not ask in such a construction how this doctrine of Paul compares with the definition of the Church in terms of a perfect society or whether or not it implies the infallibility of the Pope. One tries to bring to the text and the reconstruction of the author's thinking behind the text no questions except such as might have occurred to the author himself. (Though one grants that the author may never have tried formally to formulate a "theology" in his own mind.) Of course this level tends to extremes of multiplicity.

A third level of work on biblical theology has to do with grouping, ordering, relating elements found in the various theologies of individual authors as just described. Paul treats of the Church as the Body of Christ. To what extent is John saying the same thing when he portrays Christ's prayer that all who believe "may be one in me?" "I in them and thou in me, that they may be made perfect in unity"? Or when Mark writes Jesus' words to the paralytic "that you may know that the Son of Man has power on earth to forgive sins. . . ." Is his Son of Man, Jesus in the flesh, also meant in this story for the corporate figure of the son of man of Daniel, so that this story of the cure of the paralytic is also a hidden lesson on the Church's power to forgive sins? And is this one same Mystical Body doctrine?

The theology of the stone, the word, life, light, the body, love, dying and rising, persecution, and many many others run through most of the writers of the New Testament. And even where images change, the great subjects — God, Christ, the Spirit, covenant, circumcision, law, good and evil — remain the same. How to unify these? Is there a "message of the New Testament," a theology of the early Church presented in the New Testament as a pattern and ideal for future ages, or at least as one revelation for future ages? Is there a theology, not of John or James or Paul, but of the Author of the Bible? If so, how to find it out, how to grasp it as one whole, how to express it in words?

And ultimately, depending on the success achieved in working out the previous step, the theology of the New Testament, to be a real theology properly so called, must try to integrate the results it has obtained into one theology, one understanding of the one faith, and as much as possible into one single expression which will fit perfectly with all the rest of theology as it is known and lived in its other branches within the Church today. This theology of the New Testament must make one whole with today's dogma, first of all, but also with today's attempts to study and understand all of dogma, and finally the whole must fit in perfectly with all the rest of the Church's real and present-day life.

For no theology can be the study of curiosities from another age. It will never suffice to say, "Peter held that Christ went and preached to the spirits that were in prison." The truth expressed in that difficult passage of 1 Peter about the resurrected Christ preaching to the spirits must be, is, a truth in the Church today. Biblical theology as a fourth step must identify in the real world of today the things it has uncovered in the biblical thought-world of ancient times, and it must take a stand in regard to them. The truths — if it is a question of truths — or the attitudes or practices if that is what are concerned, have, if they are really a part of revelation, some place in the living Church today. They may exist as clearly defined dogmas, they may be in the state of popular traditions, devotional practices, or perhaps simply in the sphere of lived reaction of the Body of Christ to a hostile world. But they are there someplace, and if it is not immediately evident where, then the evidence must be examined and reexamined at both ends until it is rightly understood.

The present book, as an attempt to explain something of what New Testament theology has already accomplished and where it seems to be heading, lies somewhere between points 3 and 4 in the list of steps just given; that is, between some attempt at a unified view of what the New Testament authors are expressing in common, and the attempt to show how this common New Testament doctrine integrates with theology today. Of course there remains a vast amount of work to be done on points 1 and 2, the exact exegesis and determination of the full theological viewpoint of each single author. But a vast amount of work on points 1 and 2 has also already been done, and as a matter of fact biblical theologians are already simultaneously more and more occupying themselves with points 3 and 4.

In one sense the time is never ripe to construct and still less to put on paper a biblical theology. Evidence which touches on the very foundations is constantly coming in. A synthesis of positions which will soon be abandoned seems hardly worth making.

But at the same time, in another sense, the time is always ripe for attempting a biblical theology. For in every human investigator, consciously or unconsciously, the very gathering of material on the most fundamental levels, the work of basic exegesis itself, is always being influenced by some implicit, at least shadowy picture of the whole toward which he feels himself to be working. And the more often one attempts to bring out into the open and discuss frankly different possible pictures of the whole, of that end and goal of the process of investigation, the more solidly and scientifically the work can progress, because it will be progressing more openly and honestly, and will be more subject to needed modification and correction. No one is bound to any individual biblical theology simply because some author has attempted to put one into words. We are bound only to the word of truth as the Church delivers it to us. She alone is the final authoritative and definitive interpreter of Scripture. The synthesis toward which we are all working is that synthesis of all truth which is the living and teaching Church. But to attempt to write out that structure which seems to lie ahead, to be shaping up in the future of biblical theology, whose essential lines the biblical theology of today has already largely uncovered in the pages of Scripture, and whose substantial agreement with the living outline of the Church is already clear — this can only do good. And this is true in every age, at every stage of development of research.

For it is important to remember that the whole process of biblical theology — like that of all true theology — proceeds in faith, and from faith to faith. For theology is the understanding of the faith. And only by faith do we know or even rightly suspect in the first place that there is some one true theology to be gotten out of the New Testament. It is only because of our faith in the Church that we know the New Testament is the word and message of the God who always speaks true. It is only by that same faith that we know the writers of the New Testament are not completely disparate and divergent, contradicting one another in their accounts, propagating perhaps renegade doctrine in the midst of the community, or deceived or lying.

It is this same faith of the Church that stands behind and enforces our conviction that the New Testament has something to say which is objectively true for every generation. It is this which keeps us from being able to rest content with knowledge such as "Paul believed that there was some sort of objective connection between Christ's resurrection and our own. Because he rose, we will rise. He rose from the dead for our justification." This may be true, but so long as it is phrased simply "Paul believed," it has not yet been fully integrated into theology. We keep looking, searching for the full objective truth of the matter which the Holy Spirit is teaching us through Paul.

So again, "baptism for the dead" — if there was such a thing — cannot simply be dismissed as an aberration of the early Church. Theology is the understanding of the faith. But the faith is one, and does not admit of aberrations. What really was part of Christian faith and practice then, and really was included in Scripture as such, has something to tell us and teach us today. The same remarks could be made about baptism in the name of Jesus, healings and exorcisms, prophesying and tongues in the services, etc. If these things are mentioned in Scripture, they are there because God wanted them there, "for teaching, for reproof, for correction, and for training in righteousness . . ." (2 Tm 3, 16).

Again, it is to the Church that biblical theology looks for guidance in its attempt to insert its theological schemata, derived from the Bible, into the whole of Catholic tradition. Because of its faith in the Church, it feels the obligation to show this consonance with all tradition; and with the Church as guide, it approaches the successful fulfilling of this object.

Again, because of its faith in the Church and guided by the Church, it performs one of its most important tasks, comparing its findings with what exists in the living Church today. For, since the Church of today is the same living body which biblical theology studies in the New Testament, the same living body which produced this same New Testament as a testimony to itself under divine guidance, then the same basic features and the same life are to be found in the New Testament and in the living Church. Looking for this, picking out its outlines, will and does help in understanding the New Testament, and helps to a deeper understanding of the essential structure of the Church of today.

Again, because of its faith in the Church and the faith in the Bible which it receives from the Church, New Testament theology can never forget its responsibility to help serve the Church in her continual self-revivifying and self-rejuvenating at the font of life which is the word of God. The Church deliberately preserves Scripture for herself as a measure and norm for herself in all ages. From it she has always allowed her sincere and saintly reformers to draw, and from it many wholesome reforms have come. When the Church needs and desires them, they will continue to come — reforms like those achieved by St. Francis of Assisi, for example, inspiring himself by the simple, direct message of the gospel, and answering to the special needs of the Church at a time when many of her members, even ecclesiastics, were in their personal lives wandering away from the gospel ideal.

Classical theology has regularly drawn new life, inspiration, and self-renewal from Scripture and from the attempt to understand the Bible and its message more sharply and clearly. Biblical theology may be used again by the Church even today to point to a future reuniting of dogmatic, ascetical, mystical, moral, and liturgical theology into a single kerygmatic whole, a single whole system of theology which will leave greater room for a greater concern for Christian living, for the moving influence and power of Christian truth in every moment of Catholic living, greater than is usually able to be covered in a standard theology course today. In the original, first-generation theology of the Church, these diverse aspects of the one truth were more united because closer to the one beginning, united almost as are branches and leaves in a seed. Perhaps a renewed study of the first beginnings can lead to a greater clarification of the relations of today's elaborated parts with one another, the essential lines along which they should and must work together.

Biblical theology is, in other words, a step along the way, a part of the process, a single aspect of the production of the one perfect theology toward which all theologians constantly work. At least it is from this point of view that it has been considered and presented here.

For once one takes this approach to theology, trying to start off from the Bible, and working out from the text of Scripture itself, casting the doctrine first in strictly scriptural terms, it is inevitable that the results cover a wider amount of territory than that traditionally handled at present by what we call dogmatic theology. Biblical theology tends to include not only ascetics, moral, history of dogma, and so on, but also not a little of human psychology and daily living in the Church: Church practice and life on both the formal and organized level of liturgy, sacraments, hierarchy, as well as something of the whole range of Spirit-informed life of the practicing Christian. All these tend to enter immediately and directly into biblical theology. There is of course no intrinsic reason why they should not enter into, be considered, weighed, and formulated by dogmatic theology as well. Sometimes they are. Certainly such things have never ceased to interest many dogmatic theologians. But still, in recent centuries at least, as the vast bulk of material to be assimilated and synthesized by dogmatic theology has grown still vaster, specialization has set in, as it must in any science, and these fields have tended to be left to other specialists, known as moral or ascetic or mystical theologians, when not to pastoral helpers, canon lawyers, etc. The dogmatic theologians tended to concern themselves above all, as was indeed necessary, with those issues which had become special points of controversy with those outside the Church. Then, having once begun and achieved notable progress in those precise points they often tended to go on developing those same points in their own speculative work even after the controversy had died down. The reason is not too far to seek: the points were already at hand, and they already made part of the regular theology course that had to be handed down in the seminaries.

This tended to be less true among the medieval theologians.

The proper range of interest of the dogmatic theologians was then considered to be wider, and it could come closer to approximating the full life of the Church. Still farther back, in the patristic age, it could come closer still. One value therefore of an attempt to formulate a biblical theology is likely to be a new possibility of refreshing dogmatic theology. It may help point the way to how the speculative theologian can take for his field of study and speculation this whole wide range of interest and reality which is the Church. For God reveals and speaks to us through the whole Church. His truth is committed to the whole living structure of the Church, to each part according to its rank and function in the whole, beginning from the highest. And some of the deepest truths may even today still be being passed on by the Church through her ordinary teaching of the creed, or through the action and reaction of her whole hierarchical structure in concrete situations, through liturgical action and life, even while these are being overlooked — never of course denied — in technical dogmatic theology.

One obstacle in the way of these developments is of course that when one turns to Scripture to investigate a given dogma, and all the more when one sets out to demonstrate a thesis, one feels a constant pressure if not necessity to move away from the biblical text, to adopt indirect procedures, reinterpreting old words, changing terminology, modifying the questions asked. The Trinity, the divinity of Christ, the constitution and nature of the Church, of grace, of the sacraments — these things are present in the New Testament beyond a doubt, as sound scholars will grant. But for the most part, as we saw in Chapter 11, we do not find them being explicitly taught in the New Testament. This fact is explained, correctly, by pointing out that the New Testament writings are for the most part "occasional" writings, not theological treatises. That is, they were written amid the concerns of real life for real people, whose immediately pressing needs were not long and scientifically exact theoretical theological explanations, but practical advice and here and now consolation and encouragement. In the course of these writings much dogma is referred to, much is also clearly presupposed as learned in the original catechetical instructions of the new converts. Other points appear which have not as yet been worked out explicitly in their theoretical formulations, and which, as explicit dogmas, had still to develop. But the fact remains, the apostolic letters are not ordinarily concerned with *teaching* these things.

A complete biblical theology then, trying to reconstruct in its fullness the message of the Author, and taking the text itself as its point of departure, must at least ask itself what it is the apostolic writings were concerned with and why. And then, in the light of its faith in the inspiration of Scripture and of the importance of the canon as the word of God, must ask further whether it can safely look on the great diversity of subjects there treated as being so "occasional" after all. Did not God have his deliberate plan in all this?

True, some things must be attributed to the physical setting of the writings and certain consequent mechanical necessities. If Paul's use as a divine instrument is to be as letter writer, the letter needs a physical real-life occasion. It has to be from someone and to someone in a particular place. And hence salutations, greetings, well-wishings, requests for news, etc., are perhaps no part of a divinely planned message. But if the bulk of the letter is a request for a master to treat a slave in a certain way, or if almost half of the whole text of many letters is moral exhortation, is it safe to say or feel that this is not theology, that this is not as much as the rest a divine message to be heard and pondered and integrated with all the rest? Can one say that Romans as a speculative theological concern ends in Chapter 8 or 11 instead of in 16? Ephesians in 4 instead of 6? Is it pure accident that so much New Testament space is taken up with Jewish-Christian relations and the validity of the old law? No treatise is devoted to these questions in ordinary dogmatic theology today. Are they really only incidental?

Must we not rather suspect, at least until we have carefully investigated, that they are very important indeed if they are granted so much space in so small a volume? That they are being spoken, if not to us at least for us, and that perhaps there is a real sense in which these preoccupations might be our preoccupations too. (Perhaps this sort of an approach, followed by a careful study of the living Church, would show that they are already our concerns and preoccupations, under another name. That too we might suspect apriori.) At any rate, what one finds this way would be always something consistent with the Church as she is, and yet always too at the same time something of a warning and an encouragement and a guide for the future as the Church's understanding of Scripture, always correct and always full, always continues to deepen.

Theology, finally, all theology, is an attempt to understand. One of the most important aspects of understanding, perhaps its very essence, is the fusing into unity, seeing all as one insofar as it is one. Biblical theology finds the principle for that unified view, its basis of organization, in something directly biblical. More exactly, it seeks what Scripture presents and how Scripture unifies what it presents, and then examines whether that same principle of unity might not in practice suffice to unify all theological knowledge, even such as is not directly biblical.

Here biblical theology overlaps of course with the best of dogmatic and even scholastic theology. St. Thomas hardly considered himself a nonbiblical theologian. He taught two courses in Scripture, one in the Old Testament and one in the New, every year of his teaching career. This meant he gave two of five classes every week to direct commentary on the Bible. His dogmatic *Summa* seeks to unite the traditional organization of theology according to subject headings: God, man, grace, Christ, etc., with the biblical principle of unity through historical development according to the order of the Old and New Testaments. He wrote, moreover, that practically all of the doctrine of theology is contained in the epistles of St. Paul alone — and in the psalms of David; and, working from the text of St. Paul, he ordered theology in a way we today would call psychological and genetic, showing how the whole vast structure begins with and depends on the act of faith in Christ crucified and risen as our salvation.

Such an approach to a unifying principle is especially important if one takes a sufficiently broad view of all theology — realizing that it has to do not only with words and propositions, with true statements, but rather that it is really an attempt to understand and then to put into words the whole of Christian life, the whole of the living Church in all her richness — the Church not only teaching, but guiding, ruling, sanctifying, as well as guided, sanctified, taught, and ruled, as she really is. Theology would grasp and present all of that — if possible — and grasp it and present it all as one.

Therefore, in summary: on such and such a date and place and time, a man was killed, executed. On such and such a date and place and time, this man was seen alive again. On such and such a date and place and time, his followers, having all seen him thus alive and well, realized, grasped, had insight into, what this double fact meant — all that it implied as to who this man was, what their relations to him were, what life was all about.

From that day they began to tell others about what they had realized, basing it all on and in this tremendous double fact which they had seen and experienced, and then understood. The written records of their attempt to explain all this have come down to us in the documents of the New Testament; their fullest and most completely developed explanation we have in the gospels.

This book has been one more attempt to sum up what they said, expressing it in summary fashion, and adapting it somewhat to the thought patterns of men of this time. That has meant trying to explain at some length their original experience and insight; then passing on to how they put it into words: the immediate conclusions they drew from their insight and preached to the world. It has meant finally trying to see and show how the whole man-God relationship since then, receiving its pattern in their first divinely guided insight and preaching, has developed unchangingly along those same lines, so that all the history of the Church in the world and everything the Church has to offer today in all her being and teaching, is a true growth within one Body which existed perfect already then.

And this we take to be a biblical theology; for it is an attempt to understand God insofar as he has revealed himself to man, and therefore a theology; and it draws the main guiding lines of its research and the patterns and structures according to which it shapes its material direct from the Bible, and is therefore specifically biblical. And it concerns itself above all with showing the unity of revelation in Scripture and tradition, showing how all the life and teaching of tradition — i.e., of the living Church in all times — follows the patterns and structures laid down in the Bible.

It does not say that "Greek" categories of scholastic theology, so useful in their transtemporal and transcultural possibilities, should be replaced by "biblical" or "Semitic" categories. It does say that the relation between the two types had better be clearly established and the possibility demonstrated of reducing adequately the later Greek and scholastic categories to those of the original revelation. This becomes possible not by wrenching either, but by understanding both. If there is any question of subordination here — it may be doubted — it seems clear that the later must be subordinated to the earlier; that is, in the sense that they must be shown to agree with, be consistent with the biblical, if not perhaps by saying precisely the same thing, then at least by always serving the same purpose. Such at least is the solution suggested in Chapters 11 and 15: that the later were necessarily developed, precisely in order to safeguard the fullness, the purity, and the truth of the earlier; not to replace them, but to be, in a different age and culture, their indispensable support.

INDEX OF SCRIPTURAL PASSAGES

(Chapter numbers indicated by bold-face type; verse numbers by light-face type; page numbers by italic type.)